The Way of the Angels

A Guide to Life with the Angels

The Angel Ladies
Deborah Vaughan
Jean Porche

Gate Street Books

Angel of God, my guardian dear, to whom God's love commits me here, ever this day be at my side, to light, to guard, to rule and guide. Amen.

How very grateful we are to our loving angels who surround us with steadfast love and constant inspiration on this journey.

We dedicate this book to our family, friends and all who have helped us gain insights and understanding about our heavenly friends.

How blessed we are to do what we love.
--Deb and Jean

Contents

Part 1 – Introduction to Angels

Introduction

This e-book, presented in a three-part volume, is based on the information presented in our popular Way of the Angels Course.

In this first part, we examine Angelology, the history of angels and the way in which they have been perceived by humankind for thousands of years. We believe that for those who want to understand who and what angels are, it is important to see the way in which people have perceived and interacted with them throughout the centuries.

In the second part, we bring the angels to a much more personal level, offering ways in which to communicate with them and receive their guidance.

In the third part, we offer several meditations and talk about spiritual protection.

Using this eBook Series as a Workbook

Because this series of books is based upon our "Way of the Angels" course, you'll find that there are questions related to the material for you to think about and explore. You may find it helpful to print it out and make notes on the book as you go. Mark it up. Write questions. What seems new or odd? What do you appreciate or disagree with?

You can choose to read the book straight through without stopping to consider the reflection questions or taking time for the activities. For those who truly want the experience of the workshop, it will take a little longer to work through the chapters, but the rewards, we believe, will be worth the effort.

Tools for the Journey

Getting a dedicated notebook or journal of some kind will be extraordinarily helpful. Most chapters will contain one or more journal questions, which you can elect to complete. It is entirely up to you.

Journaling is a wonderful practice. Your journal will become your record of the journey you begin with the first part of the book. Much of it is informational, but there will be places to stop and see what is resonating with your understanding of angels.

In the second part especially, your journal will become the place where you and your angel meet and where, afterward, you'll reflect on the teachings and guidance you receive. Because it is your journal, there is no special method or process to follow. Follow your heart and write what you will.

This journey is a mystic's path. Looking back on the steps you've taken, as recorded in your journal, will be extremely helpful. The insights you gain today will yield new and deeper insights next week, next month, next year.

If you are not a regular journal-keeper, please do not look upon this as a burden. Your journal will be a very precious document. It is a gift you make to yourself.

To heighten your experience, there are recorded guided meditations that are available for download on mp3 at www.theangel-ladies.com to help you become more aware of your angels and begin to work with them.

Chapter 1 - A Long-Standing Love Affair with Angels

People are fascinated by the subject of angels. In our more than 20 years working together, we have heard amazing stories of angelic encounters and have met people who spend their days surrounded by reminders of their heavenly friends.

We have discovered that angels are a universal symbol of protection and goodness and so transcend any one religion or spirituality. In fact, many people who have no faith tradition at all report that they believe in angels. A recent poll involving a cross section of Americans from all walks of life and backgrounds reported that eight out of ten of them believed in angels.

This is significant.

We live in a society that is rapidly changing. Our world can often feel as though we move from crisis to crisis. Our religious institutions, once the sure-fire havens of comfort and acceptance, are also in transition, shaken by horrendous scandals and changing attitudes. Our financial security is threatened both personally and globally as the economy rollercoasters and countries across the world struggle to stay afloat. Earth itself is in crisis, with its very survival – and ours – uncertain.

Our way of looking at the world is shifting as we are bombarded by instant images and information taking place in faraway places. And, as we absorb news of violence, terrorism, disasters and any number of events, we are impacted by every negative action, word and image in a very deep way.

It is no wonder that we look for a force that can work to assist us personally and directly. For many people God is a very distant and immensely preoccupied CEO of the universe. An angel, however, is a personal and immediate friend.

It is our hope that this e-book will help you understand more fully the unlimited power that is available to you through the angels given to you by our loving Creator and bring you a sense of peace and hope in the midst of the storms that rage around us.

Our Understanding

We believe that an angel is an agent of God, of Divine Will. Angels are in existence because Creator loves us so much that angels are sent as a gift to assist us as we journey through our lives. An angel is Creator's love and grace in action, a force of light and goodness, sent to help us.

Everyone comes to understand about angels in their own time, at a pace that is right for them. Some people will never get to the point where angels are more than a nice figure to put atop a Christmas tree, and that is fine. Angels are with us and here to help us whether we believe they exist or not.

We've both had very different experiences of the angelic world and those insights have brought us together to teach and help people gain understanding about the angels in their life. Here is a little about each of us and our take on the angelic world.

Deb's Story:

I've always been fascinated with the unseen world. All through my life, I was aware that there were things that happened that I couldn't explain but knew were more than my imagination. As early as high school, I was curious about things like astrology and numerology and read lots of books about the paranormal, but many of the ideas were way too big to wrap my head around at that ripe young age. I have discovered that there are always ideas that stretch us beyond the limit of our knowledge and experience

– and that is exciting indeed!

Later, in college, I remember late night talks over wine with my friends, trying to sort out the universe. I remember a Monty Python song that began, "Oh, God, you are so big..." and that's basically how I saw God - as a limitless, elusive cosmic puzzle. It hurt my brain to think so deeply!

When I was in my twenties, I found myself attending church regularly again for the first time since I was a young teen. There was something about the mystery and the liturgy and the community and the clergy... a combination that seemed quite magical and it satisfied something within that was really thirsting. So much so, that I went back to university and became a priest in the Anglican church.

Almost 40 years later, I know it wasn't just the church experience that satisfied that thirst for God. My time at seminary and in ministry served as a springboard for my own journey of deep connection with the Divine.

Everything happens in the fullness of time. And for me, all those years being priest never prepared me for the delightful surprises and insights that came to me as my spirituality evolved. They didn't cover angels in theological courses and perhaps that aspect of spirituality should be addressed as clergy are being formed. Modern-day clerics tend not to share my enthusiasm for spiritual practices beyond the authorized prayerbook.

And yet, here we all are, having a very spiritual experience in this amazing life. The mystics knew and so do millions of people who seek deeper truths beyond the religious dogmas and doctrine. We are spiritual beings seeking an understanding of who we are and what it means for us to be here on this planet at this place in time. That is a holy and wonderful journey.

Jean's Story:
I've always been different, to put it kindly. My earliest recollec-

tion of experiencing God is of a time when I was about four or five - I know because I was wearing my forest-green wool sweater, an itchy garment beloved for its rich colour. I was in my backyard, on our 'hill' (South Louisiana has no hills, but my dad had ordered a truckload of topsoil to fill a low spot on our property; my sister and I immediately declared the mound of dirt our hill and, well, the yard never did get leveled out...*s*).

It was autumn and I suppose a front was moving into the area, because it was a grey, cloudy day, quite windy. And for me, twirling atop the hill, sweater and hair blowing hard...why, I was dancing with God. The wind was God, in my mind.

I've spent my life trying to get back to that hill.

Needless to say, 'God = Wind' was not a concept the good sisters who taught me at the Catholic school endorsed. It would be fairer to say it was one they strenuously unendorsed! Along with many of my ideas...even at the young age of seven, I was making nuns twitch when I asked, "Why can't I be Roman Catholic AND Jewish? Jesus was Jewish... And my uncle is Lutheran! Why can't I be all three? God doesn't care..."

Although I discovered that I was only allowed one religious faith, the nuns taught us about our Guardian Angels. One sister, who had a particular devotion to the Holy Guardian Angels, encouraged us to get to know our heavenly friend.

Being a literal kid, I immediately christened my angel John, because he (all things holy were male in our Roman Catholic vision back then) was a gift from God. And since I knew about friends, I treated John as one, chatting through the day and such. It was no surprise when John answered me, and no surprise when John did favours for me - friends do such things, don't they?

When I got older, I understood that my experience was not the norm. Like Deb, I sought other ways to make sense of spirit and the world. I bought my first deck of Tarot cards around age eleven, to my mother's dismay, and learned palm-reading and casting natal charts.

It's hard to go your own way spiritually, though -groups are far more comfortable! So I periodically forswore all my occult interests and tried hard to be a good Catholic girl. I joined the charismatic renewal sweeping through the church, I taught in Catholic schools and even spent time in a convent, trying my vocation. I couldn't reconcile the old traditions and rejection of the world with my vision of a loving God, though, and didn't enter. Instead, I became director of religious ed for the largest parish in the diocese, training religion teachers and doing sacramental preparation, etc.

But it's hard to go someone else's way spiritually - especially when you have a track record like mine, dancing with God and bickering with Jesus and sharing secrets with angels. The path led me gently to my role not as a nun but as an Angel Lady spiritually dancing on that long-ago hill.

How We See the Angels

When we researched the material for our book *Angels Help Us: Discovering Divine Guidance,* we read dozens of books and visited all kinds of websites to see what other people were saying about their experience of the angelic world. There are diverse viewpoints about angels out there, some of which seemed outlandish to us.

One of the things we noticed is how very complicated people like to make angels sound. There are these intricate charts, trees and graphs, many offering strange-sounding names for particular angels. They encourage one to call on this angel for this specific need or call on that one because it is Tuesday, or better yet, call this phone number and someone will interpret the angel for you for a fee. It all seems so complex and difficult to negotiate. For us, this is a problem.

We encourage people to take what resonates and use your intuition. We are of the belief that it just isn't all this complicated. The angels have told us that we humans have a way of overdoing things and quite miss the point of it all. They are here to help us any way that they can and bring us a sense of peace. That is basically the job description of an angel.

We both come at this from traditional faith traditions, which we love. Our studies have given us a breadth of knowledge from which to approach the study of angels in a very grounded and structured way. This is not to discount the revelations and understandings of others at all, but it does mean that people who cannot understand or accept some of the New Age visions of angels and spiritualities may find here a comfortable place from which to begin their exploration.

At the same time, both of us have found traditional expressions of faith to be rather constricting for the experiences we have had of divinity in our lives. For that reason, we are not willing to approach the study of angels from a dogmatic perspective, ie., WE have the One Truth!

Angels predate the creation of religions, and so we will not take the study of angels from any one religious perspective, although we will consider various religious understandings. We take the standpoint that to the One Divine there are many paths, and it is for each person to discover the path by which he or she may most profitably come to understand God.

Because the largest body of angelic information in the West is found in the Judeo-Christian religious traditions, you'll find we speak of these more than others. The holy books of the Judeo-Christian traditions have much to say of angels, their roles, and their relationship to people.

We believe it is important to share the angelic understandings of other religious or philosophical traditions. We will not express any one of these traditions as the 'correct' one; our perspective is that each is correct for someone and has truths to share with everyone. Universal truths.

Here, we will treat the stories from the holy books of all faiths as stories, nothing more. This does not mean we do not respect and honour them, nor is this intended to be an expression of our personal belief systems.

Truth is Truth on Many Levels

We have come to understand that Truth is multi-layered; while we may not be a member of the Hindu faith and share belief in the gods of that tradition, we may still learn much of value from that faith. Further, the truths we find in that faith will be mirrored in the Christian tradition, the Jewish tradition, the Islamic tradition, and in various New Age and New Thought traditions as well.

For the purposes of this book, treating all holy books as faith-stories and myth allows us to discuss the truths contained in each without getting bogged down in discussions of religious doctrines - that old 'Mine is right!' 'No, MINE is!' kind of religious conversation.

We leave it to each person to decide the religious or historical truth of any holy book. Please do not be offended by our approach; we respect all traditions, but we do not want to be in the business of promoting any one of them. We serve Love.

Chapter 2 – Life is the Cherries, Spirit is the Bowl...

Let's begin this chapter by looking at a subject that is near and dear to us all: Life. It is something we all share in common, yet our experiences are vastly unique and different. So, consider for a moment. How does life feel for you? What have you observed about life? Are you happy?

For the vast majority of North Americans, life is work, lots of it, and precious little return on the investment. Sounds harsh? Think for a moment.

Most people live paycheck to paycheck. Few people have even one month's salary in their savings accounts in case of emergency. Debt is at an all-time high for both consumers and government. Finances are the number one cause of argument and marital discord.

As if that wasn't bad enough, few people have the luxury of going to a job they like, much less one that is a joy for them. Each workday takes them to a place of business where they are not affirmed, not supported, not welcomed. Their workloads far exceed the rate of compensation they receive; many jobs include a competitive element that creates a never-ending stress as new workers come on board looking to move up and make job security elusive.

Perhaps you know of someone who has lost a job because of outsourcing by a company to workers in foreign land. Maybe you've been downsized. The days of staying with the same job through to retirement are over and done, it would seem.

And let's not forget getting to that job – commuting is not only time-consuming, it's becoming dangerous as well. Traffic accidents, dangerous highway pollution, and now road rage and random violence troubling even smaller communities... it's a hard road, all right.

Moms have an especially difficult time of it. If they work outside the home, they face all the above, plus the cost and guilt of day-care. If they don't work outside the home, there is the financial stress of a one-income family. If they work inside the home, they face an entirely different set of stressors that bear on the matter. And if they are single moms, their lives have challenges we cannot begin to detail.

And that's just work! Home life is challenging, too. Adults find themselves juggling schedules, commitments, extracurricular activities for children, housekeeping details, shopping, laundry, aging parents, and more.

By the time most folks fall into bed, they're exhausted on every level - physical, mental, emotional, and spiritual. And when the sun rises, it's time to start it all over again.

You may think weekends offer the time needed to recuperate from all that work, but most people use weekends for catching up on the work that didn't get completed during the workweek. Those who aren't busy with catch-up chores often spend weekends in a frantic quest for relaxation that leaves them tired and exhausted when Monday rolls around again. There's never any time, it seems, although we may not be sure what we want that time for, anymore.

It's a rut, all right, and often the only thing that disturbs the sameness is a crisis (good or bad) that excites a flurry of new activity until it is met – and then life settles down into that same old rut.

Most people suffer from at least a low-grade depression, we read, and given the scenario, it would be hard to imagine anyone escaping the aching feeling of futility. They call it 'the grind' for a reason; it really is a daily grind - and sadly, what gets ground most often is US.

When life lacks satisfaction, our jobs, our health, our relationships - they all suffer. When life seems driven by deadlines, obligations, the shoulds and musts and gottas of other people's agendas, peace flees. The future, by contrast, may seem to be a far-off Someday Paradise where things will be better. So we buy lottery tickets and pray, indulging in a bit of daydreaming of a life far happier than the present circumstances allow.

Life is real, life is earnest, but it sure isn't much fun.

Where are you in this bleak scenario? Perhaps some of it sounds familiar; we hope it doesn't describe your life today, but there are probably parts of it that you know from experience.

This is not how life is meant to be. Such lives may be dutiful and sincere, such people may generously give their happiness in exchange for the necessities of their families, but this is not the abundant life we are called to embrace.

If life is as unbalanced as the unhappy picture depicts, it lacks the vitality that marks life itself. That vitality, the spark that puts life into our lives, is spirituality. By spirituality, we do not mean the exercise of a particular religion, although for many people such exercises are powerful expressions of their spirituality. We mean the care and nurture of the spirit that lives in each of us.

Call in the Angels
Angels help up put life into our lives. Simply by acknowledging their existence, we express our recognition that there is more to life than what we see. In this simple act, we open the way to an expanded vision of life and living.

This expanded vision is called mysticism. Mysticism refers to the direct personal experience of the Divine. Mysticism has gotten a bad rap over the years; in ancient years it was associated with mystery schools whose teachings sometimes contradicted that of the dominant religions of the day.

For our purposes, though, we will limit our definition of mysticism to the direct personal experience of the Divine.

Angels open our eyes to the action of God in the world. When we perceive the movement of Love through the world, it can be a transcendent moment, a moment of connection and union with All that Is. And, while our focus is angels, we can never forget that THEIR focus is always and forever, Love.

Once we recognize part of this unseen world, we are forever changed.

Journal questions:
What mystical experiences have you had? When have you experienced Love, God, the Angels, Loved Ones, etc., in intensely powerful or personal ways?

Chapter 3 - An Awareness of the Angelic Realm

There are many ways in which people connect with the invisible world. Near-death experiences, for example, are a powerful experience of the continuation of life after the body has died. Visitations from departed loved ones, little signs of their continued interest in and love for us alert many to the expanded world. It may be as simple as a child twirling in the wind, joyfully dancing with God.

Angels help us recognize and discern the mystical experiences that come to us. They alert us to God's action in us, through us, and around us. The experience of transcendence often takes us into one of sublime union. That is, the experience of rising beyond the ordinary to an extraordinary experience of Love takes us to an expanded vision of the ordinary, physical world - to a vision of the world that reveals divinity through every created thing.

Through our union with the divine, then, we become aware of our union with all that is, the family of humans, as it were.

There is a question that we like to pose to people. "How many angels do YOU have?" Chances are, if you are like most folks, you have a guardian angel pin or a mantelpiece collection of angels or know someone who does. The idea of the heavenly friend who watches over each of us from birth to death brings great comfort to people, especially those in pain or distress of any kind.

At the same time, as we look on that little angel on the shelf, it takes us into a realm of the unseen, the unknown, the divine. It invites us to think about the presence of something greater than ourselves-- which can be daunting for our limited imagination and self-worth.

Many of us on the spiritual journey have a difficult time accepting the angelic hand, so to speak. And for many who struggle, accepting that hand is the first step in accepting the God they cannot understand.

People may consider the interest in angels to be a feature of our time but from the beginning of recorded history – and before that, as ancient prehistoric relics have revealed – early peoples recognized the reality of both a Creator and the winged beings who attended that Divine Source.

Angels Across Time and Borders

Around the world, cultures from the most primitive to the most sophisticated shared several common features: a belief in the importance of family, a belief in some kind of higher power, and a belief in heavenly messengers who attend the creator and assist humans.

When we find such a connection shared across time and culture, we take it seriously. For us, it is a sign of a deep truth instinctively realized within the human spirit.

Jung referred to archetypes, or symbolic figures that reflect aspects of the human subconscious that are common to many diverse cultures. Many believe, as we do, that angels fall into this category, along with such concepts as mother, hero, seeker, villain. With their wings at the ready to fly into our lives and assist, Angels are a universal symbol heavenly support, guidance and protection.

The power of symbol often gives voice to something deeper than words, something we immediately recognize and to which we can instantly relate. As the human family we all share the same needs, the same questions and the same desire for fulfillment and love.

Our experiences may vary but at the heart of it all we are all here on this planet to build happy and purposeful lives. And we all have the same quest to know the answers to the big questions: why am I here? What is this life? Is there more after death?

The unknown has always fascinated humans, whether it is the cycle of day and night or the flicker of fire or the existence of a Supreme Being and how we interact with that Creator. Angels share the aura of mystery, the glow of divinity, and so occupy the minds and hearts of humans. It is as natural for us today to ponder their existence, wondering what messages they bring, as it was thousands of years ago for humans to gaze into the heavens and ponder the origins of the starry sky.

Early people decorated their caves with the things they knew: a hunt, the animals they observed, tribal ceremonies and rituals, and sometimes, angels. The earliest civilizations, which gave rise to the winged gods of Greek and Egyptian religions, displayed angelic figures on stone cylinder seals and on steles or stone panels.

An early angel carving, circa 4000 B.C.E., shows an angel sharing the water of life with an earthly ruler, into whose upheld cup the angel pours it. Even then, angels were seen as intermediaries between the divine and the human.

From the beginning of time and culture, people have sought to define and understand the bridge between human and divine. They intuitively understood that there were beings higher than humans and lower than God, beings whose purpose was to somehow connect us, to bring messages and guidance, a two-way communication.

As groups of people organized into towns and nations, the emphasis shifted to power and wealth, giving rise to the argumentative and power-hungry gods of ancient Greece and Egypt. Lesser gods and goddesses, frequently winged beings, functioned as messengers or intermediaries. Even today, floral offerings from loved ones are delivered by the winged messenger's modern counterparts at FTD!

In the various cultures, these intermediaries and winged beings were not always called "angels." They were gods and demi-gods, Isis and Nike and Cupid. They were Eagle and Raven, the messengers to the aboriginal peoples. From the Greek that we get our word "Angel," from that language's 'Angelos,' meaning messenger.

In Judaism, Christianity and Islam we find angelic messengers who share the goal of helping and protecting us. In fact, these three religions have angels in common, notably Gabriel, who brought a revelation to Muhammad and thereby sparked the basis for Islam.

When we examine who and what angels are, we find very diverse ideas. For some, angels walk the earth, being incarnated as humans and living lives as Earth Angels- humans descended from the realms of glory to experience life on earth. Others see angels as energy forms, much like thoughts or emotions, that spring from the Divine. Still others see angels as other-worldly life forms, misunderstood by humans to be messengers from the Divine but in actuality, simply advanced beings.

Others regard departed loved ones, especially children, as angels in heaven. Many consider angels merely a metaphor for our conscience or higher self. And there are those who put angels in the same box as Santa Claus or the Tooth Fairy: a comforting character of legend and myth, no more real than the Easter Rabbit with its basket of candy eggs.

Chapter 4 - Angels in Early Cultures

Across the spectrum of faith, from the earliest of times to the present, through diverse cultures and lands, angels are recognized as emanating from God. Good angels are recognized as carrying out God's directives and assisting humans, while fallen angels or demons tempt people to sin.

It can be argued that when an idea is found in such widely disparate cultures and philosophies, that idea contains some truth which has been divinely revealed or intuitively understood by humans despite their differences.

The fact that angels appear in such number in so many cultures and faiths speaks to us of God revealing holy truths to us, God's children. The details differ, true; but in one essential area, there is accord: Angels are.

Thousands of years before Christ, the earliest societies, matriarchal in structure, revered a loving earth-mother goddess and flowed with the natural rhythm of the planet. In these tightly-knit communities, where leadership was shared and equality was the keynote of life, so too did their theology embrace not a single goddess, but many. Birth, death, regeneration: cycles of life, like the seasons of the year, mirrored the qualities of deity.

Along with the earth-mother goddess, they recognized other goddesses with specific duties. Some of these goddesses were winged like birds. Their duties included delivering souls into the afterlife and transmitting prophetic messages to the humans who sought their counsel.

The Egyptians, Romans, Greeks, Sumerians and Babylonians were all birthed from similar matriarchal roots which saw deity in the cycle of the seasons and in the patterns of the stars. As each nation developed, shaped by their own distinctive worldview, their understanding of the cosmos matured and developed, but the original connection to divinity and the natural order remained.

And so it is that among the various religions there were gods and goddesses who share parallel roles and yet have different names. This is especially noticeable in the similarities between Greek deities and their Roman counterparts such as Eros and Cupid, gods of love, and Artemis and Diana, goddesses of the hunt.

These cultures saw the most important of their deities --Zeus, Amon-Ra, Osiris, Apollo--as being largely uninvolved and disinterested in mere mortals. Lesser gods and goddesses were in charge of weather, cycles of the seasons, the well-being of all living things, and the care and guidance of men and woman. Many of the deities, such as Nike, Mercury, Osiris, and Cupid were winged and acted as messengers between the divine and the created order.

The Greeks, the Romans and the Egyptians also believed in personal spirits that were rather like a guardian angel, assigned to each person at birth. To the Greek, this special spirit was called a daimon; to the Roman, this attending being was known as genius; and to the Egyptians they were known as ba or ka.

Not only did the literature and story of these various cultures have an impact on world history, but some philosophical perspectives have influenced the minds of humanity for thousands of years. The Greek philosophers Plato and Aristotle, who revolutionized rational thinking in the second century BCE, greatly inspired the founders of the early church who were Greek-speaking and familiar with Hellenistic society.

After the death of Christ, the early Christians, whose understanding of God was based on the monotheistic roots of Judaism and the teachings of Jesus, ventured forth into the larger world where they encountered Greeks, Romans, Egyptians and others whose belief systems differed from their own.

The churches founded by Paul had to clarify and deliberate on many critical issues as the gentile world collided with long-rooted practices of the Jewish faith.

The missionaries encountered many perceptions and questions which helped define the doctrine of the early church. But the new converts had little difficulty embracing the message they heard of Christ, nor did they discount the notion of heavenly messengers or angelic assistants, for this was a familiar theme in most religious understandings.

Along the way, many of the older, local traditions and customs were assimilated into the practices of the early church. The rituals of cultures were difficult to erase and change, so missionaries applied Christian meanings over the existing celebrations and festivals known and loved by the people in each place.

Hence some of the most beloved Christian celebrations, including Christmas and Easter, are based on older pagan rituals and given a theological meaning. For example, the coming of the Son of God at the darkest point of the year, the light of Christ, and the star of Bethlehem gave new meaning to the ancient Solstice observances.

Did you ever wonder why we paint eggs and have chocolate bunnies at Easter? Easter, once the goddess of fertility, whose festival was held in the Spring with the cycle of new life, now lent her name to celebrate the new life won for believers by Christ through his passion, death and resurrection. Over the centuries, the Christian church took on flavours from many regions and religions, even as it left its Judaic roots further and further behind.

Chapter 5 - Angels in Other Religions and Traditions

For those who espouse any particular denomination, it may seem odd to think that angels had a hand in starting other religions. Nevertheless, angels are credited with having a hand in the beginnings of both Islam and Mormonism. Angel Gabriel, who visited Mary, is said to have dictated the Koran, Islam's holy book, to Mohammad. Joseph Smith said he received the Book of Mormon from an angel named Moroni.

Most religious denominations recognize angels among the heavenly citizens. Billy Graham wrote of them, as did Charles Capps. The Catholic church, often criticized for recommending its followers to ask favours of both Saints and Angels as well as the Creator, has a long tradition of interaction with angelic beings. Joan of Arc heard angels; it was an angel who brought St. Catherine Laboure to the lap of Mary in the silence of her convent's chapel.

Recently canonized St. Pio of Pietrelcina, also known as Padre Pio, spoke to the guardian angels of those who sought confession with him. Every pope since Pope Pius XI, who died in 1939, has spoken of the angels, asking that the faithful seek their help in remaining true to Love and in the trials of life.

While many consider angels to be rather New-Agey, the truth is that angels are far older than the scriptures themselves.

Because of the strong Christian influence in the West, it surprises many to realize that angels or their counterparts appear in all major religions. Instead of being confined to the Jewish and Christian experience, angels are everywhere. In fact, you'd be hard pressed to find a religion or a spiritual perspective that didn't have within its tradition stories of angels or beings who perform the functions of angels.

While the Christian "angel" derives from "angelos," a Greek word meaning messenger, other names for angels include the Persian "angaros" (courier) and the Hebrew word "malakh" (messenger). Our Western understanding of angels reflects the attributes of helping, instructing, and guiding humans as well as bringing messages from deity, and so does the understanding of every major religion, whether they are referred to as angels or as some other divine or semi-divine being. In every case, humans have a holy source of assistance as they traverse their earthly journey.

The Hindu religion of India, the oldest of the world's major religions, does not recognize angels as we do. Instead, it recognizes a host of divine figures from major gods and goddesses to minor gods, demigods, spirits, and attendants. Small towns and even households have their celestial watchers and protectors, the grama-devata, sometimes translated as the village angel.

While an overview of Hinduism is complex for the non-initiate to comprehend, the theology for the practitioner is simple: everything is connected and united in the one Source, the one God. All of the various gods, goddesses, village-angels, and diverse celestial beings are all parts of the One. In devotees' spiritual journeys, powers that help or hinder progress are regarded as angels or demons, guides or tempters.

Hinduism does not recognize the duality of good and evil, all things being part of the One. Therefore, dark angels, often a source of concern for Christians, are regarded in Hinduism as simply opportunities for growth and learning and have value as teachers who enhance the spiritual development of the faithful.

Buddhism recognizes several realms of existence. In them are many demi-gods who like our angels, are able to assist or help humans. Bodhisattvas, who may be
heavenly beings or humans, also fill some of the roles of angels. Bodhisattva means, "whose essence is enlightenment," and these beings are great in love and compassion. Some forms of Buddhism, such as Tantric Buddhism, also recognize many of the same celestial beings as the Hindus.

Zoroastrianism, while not a major religion today, is worth considering as it heavily influenced Judaism, Islam, and Christianity. Zoroaster, also known as Zarathustra, developed this religion sometime around 600 B.C.E. from an earlier Persian religion which was very similar to Hinduism in that it was polytheistic and sacrificed animals.

In fact, some of this religion's demigods share the same names as Hindu celestial beings and Zoroastrian angels, thus Zoroastrianism forms a bridge between the major religious thought of that time and the Western religions to come.

Zoroastrianism is monotheistic and dualistic, accepting both good and evil. The Great Lord, in his fight against the evil spirit Ahriman, is assisted by seven heavenly beings called the amesha spentas, the "beneficent immortals." The amesha spentas are similar in function to Western archangels. People prayed to them for help, as well as to fravishis, who acted as guardian angels.

The Torah is filled with the actions of angels, mentioning seven archangels and calling four of these by name. Judaism's angelic cast also includes evil angels and demons such as Leviathan the sea-dragon. Judaism's mysticism is embodied in the Kabbala, which means "received tradition." The knowledge contained in the Kabbala is considered to have been given to Moses at the time of the Ten Commandments and has been carefully preserved through oral tradition.

Have you ever seen cartoons depicting a person with an angel on one shoulder and a devil on the other? You may be interested to know that Kabbalists believe that each human being is attended by both an angel and a demon who may influence his or her choices in moral dilemmas, thus giving us not only a personal guardian angel but also a personal tempter!

Islam also holds that each person is attended by both guardian angels who protect him or her as well as recording angels who write down each person's good and bad acts to be used on Judgment Day. According to Islam, there are innumerable angels since Mohammad taught that every single creation, even a raindrop, is attended by an angel.

Among the non-mainstream Christian denominations, angels are recognized although they may be viewed in a slightly different manner. Moroni, for example, is the angel who instructed Joseph Smith in the location of the gold plates which he translated into the Book of Mormon. The marked the beginnings of the Church of Jesus Christ of Latter Day Saints which Smith founded after Moroni's first appearance to him in 1823. Moroni, however, was once a man on earth.

The idea of humans becoming angels after death is not a new one, as some Jewish traditions hold that the extraordinary holy men Enoch and Elijah ascended into heaven without dying and became angels. Moroni, however, is one of what Mormonism recognizes as a "re-embodied angel," that is, an angel who was originally a human being, but who died and became an angel before taking on a body in which he appeared to Joseph Smith.

Mormons also recognize "disembodied" angels who never incarnated on earth but were created by God before humans. Disembodied angels are either divine or infernal, depending on whether they serve God or Satan.

The theology of the Jehovah's Witnesses also includes the belief in angels. They name demons the wicked angels who rebelled along with Satan. Seraphs and cherubs they include among the order of angels. Based on their reading of Thessalonians and Jude, however, they include Jesus in that number, regarding him as the foremost angel, Archangel Jesus Christ, also called Michael, who rules over the seraphs, cherubs, and angels.

In 1866, Mary Baker Eddy founded the Church of Christ, Scientist. In her vision, angels are "God's thoughts passing to man; spiritual intuitions, pure and perfect...." While she saw a vision in which science and faith married, it was incomplete without angels as well.

Chapter 6 - Angels Across the Centuries

One of the most fascinating research we carried out for our **Angels Help Us** book was plotting a timeline from the time of Christ to the present. We looked at the major events happening in each century and how angels were perceived through art and expression. It was interesting to see how perception of angels shifted with the transitions and developments in the world.

Through the turbulent years of the first millennium after the death of Jesus, angels were found in the churches and cathedrals as part of great carvings and mosaics which served the illiterate faithful as both entertainment and catechism.

Much of the most beautiful angelic artwork was held in palaces and therefore inaccessible to the common people, enjoyed by nobility and those who had resources to sponsor budding artists. Other work, done in monasteries by scribes and artists, was also unavailable to ordinary people.

It was only in the churches that the people could see depictions of Bible stories, of the lives of the saints, and of the actions of angels in Scripture. They were fascinated by angels.

The Middle Ages
During the Middle Ages (the time between the 5th and 14th Centuries), philosophers and theologians searched holy writings to determine the origin of angels. Some argued that God created only the highest angels who then created the lower orders, while others looked to apocryphal Judaic writings which taught that God created the angels immediately before creating the earth.

In keeping with the hard times of the Middle Ages, angels were stern-faced figures. Sometimes they were shown with wings and other times not, depending on the artist. And, as the church followed the patriarchal thinking that had guided the Jewish faith for so long, angels were male figures, usually shown as young men of nobility and resolve.

The Renaissance

During the Renaissance (roughly 1350-1700), angels took on a new appearance and a new popularity. In an age dedicated to learning and beauty, angels were shown more softly. Their faces are depicted as compassionate and, increasingly, feminine. They are garbed in gowns of fabulous colour, in flowing Renaissance style, and often sport halos and wings. Now cherubs, those pure and innocent angel babes, gain popularity along with Christmas creche scenes. The famous "winged heads" of angels also made their appearance during this age to represent the angels' great intellect and wisdom.

Historically, this period was turbulent. The rise and fall of the Inquisition, the burning of Joan of Arc, the clash of great political powers throughout Europe, and the formation of the Church of England are among the trials that shook the very foundations of people's lives and faith.

Explorers such as Columbus, Magellan, de Gama, Cartier, and Henry Hudson helped to map a world far larger than they could comprehend. Sciences flowered as Copernicus, Gutenberg, da Vinci, Kepler, and Harvey brought forth new theories and inventions with what must have seemed incredible power.

While the Church took on heresies in terrifying purges, art became the safe place where people could take comfort in the truths they held dear. Masterpieces were produced by some of the world's greatest artists: Leonardo da Vinci, Michelangelo, Botticelli, Fra Angelico, Raphael. Chaucer, Boccaccio, and Dante completed their masterworks.

The church had been the keeper of knowledge prior to this time, when education was reserved for the clergy and the wealthy alone. Now, the invention of the printing press made learning available to anyone who could learn to read. New secular schools offered unheard-of opportunities, ending the power of the church to control the flow and discussion of ideas.

For the first time, large numbers of people no longer accepted the church as the final authority on all things. In response, the church promoted harsh orthodoxy, and men like Galileo were prosecuted and condemned by the Holy Office in Rome.

And during this period of creativity and backlash, angels gained new popularity. Serene and patient, they were a link to a loving God who must have seemed far from the action and reaction of that time. It is not by accident that one of the most popular subjects for artists of the day was the Annunciation, in which the Archangel Gabriel tells a frightened young girl that God has a plan and purpose for her life.

The angel's reassurance was as greatly needed by Renaissance commoners as it ever was by the Blessed Virgin Mary, whose calm faith and quiet acceptance of the life-changing news heralded by the angel offered great comfort to those whose very world was in flux.

Angels took a backseat for a century or so, as society assimilated the tremendous changes wrought by the Renaissance. Human rationalism and philosophy took the forefront, bringing with them the Reformation and an expanding merchant class. Increasingly, the bourgeoisie was recognizing its own power, and everything seemed to be in question: so many churches, each asserting its claim to the One Truth.

The Enlightenment
So many new philosophers throwing off the yokes of both church and aristocracy and demanding freedom and respect. And so was ushered in the Enlightenment, with its emphasis on personal equality and freedom.

Now come the revolutions - American and French – as colonists question the right of Europeans to command and order their lives. Even the right of the churches to Christianize the peoples of far-away lands came under the gun. And in the increasing focus on what was here and how, visible and provable, angels became a leftover of another time. Religious art continued to depict angels, of course, but the Renaissance ardor was gone.

The Victorian Era

By the middle of the 19th Century, the world was again in the throes of big changes. Telephone and telegraph brought the far-away into people's towns and homes. Photographers recorded events around the world, making it smaller yet. It was the age of Darwin and the Communist Manifesto, the American Civil War and the Industrial Revolution. Change - on a massive and sometimes brutal scale.

Newspapers brought detailed battlefield reports of war's realities - along with many photos of its horrors - into living rooms. Dickens outraged a nation by his depiction of the underbelly of the Industrial Revolution: child labour, poverty, pollution and homelessness - and inspired a social conscience.

Everything was changing! Beliefs and ways of being that had been accepted for a thousand years were overcome by the power of a mechanized era. Science was changing philosophy and issuing challenges even to Christianity's most sacred beliefs, such as Creation, with the new batch of -isms: deism, agnosticism, atheism, and more.

The Victorians took their search for truth beyond the doors of churches. Spiritualism, with its table tipping and séances, created sensations as people sought ways to interact directly with the divine, unfettered by the rules of the church. In this time of individual determinism, more and more people questioned whether the church had the whole truth - or any truth at all.

Where to find comfort but in those elements that endure forever - the comforts of home and family? And so the Victorians embraced family life in a way no generation before had done, filling homes with beautiful objects from the corners of the earth, celebrating birthdays and holidays with party and song.

Now Christmas comes to the fore, replacing Easter as the major holyday of the people's year. Christmas trees take their place in the home each year along with elaborate stable scenes - both topped, of course, with angels. Victorian angels abounded: cherubs and archangels, guardians protecting their charges at play, flower-decked beautiful angels with eyes cast to heaven.

The Victorian Era is parent to our own, which holds so many Victorian ideas about the power of the individual, justice and equality, the rights of all people. And like the Victorians, good people of our own time continue to work for full equality among all peoples, for faith amid the rapid development of the sciences with their near-daily revelations, and for understanding in a universe far more vast than even Verne imagined.

Twentieth Century

The twentieth century, witness to two incredibly destructive wars within the first half alone, sought peace in Victorian morality and emphasized duty over personal happiness. The second half of the century was rocked by war of a different kind as the Cold War became a constant presence in the minds of the world. Science, developing at warp speed, made progress and convenience synonymous, giving rise to a materialism never seen before.

The children of this era, rejecting the rule-bound societal values, rebelled with a way of life that shocked their elders, a way marked by individual choice in matters of faith, family, work, and morals. Growing technology, from transistors to computers, further blasted the facade of middleclass placidity as change took place at rates that defied the ordinary person's understanding or ability to assimilate.

The first half of the twentieth century relegated angels to an old religious idea no longer very relevant. After the second world war, angels took on a new role in the social consciousness.

People now viewed angels as active beings who could not only help them but befriend them as well. Angels sailing on UFOs, angels ushering in the Age of Aquarius or the Ascension, angels as sprite and fairy - the individualism of the age became an overlay of the old understanding of angel.

Previous ages sought understanding of the angels from religion. This new generation, in rejecting much of the religious expression and social rules of those earlier times, they rejected much of the religious understanding around the angels, too, choosing instead to view angels through the lens of personal interest and preference.

Further, angels moved from the church to the marketplace. Consumerism in America had been growing following the end of WWII, and now, the popularity of angels gave rise to a host of angel-themed products and gifts. Just as earlier generations sought comfort from angels in religious settings, the new generation found comfort in angel-themed items in their home.

Like our counterparts through the ages, we join the endless quest for comfort amid chaos, for truth in the face of confusion, for love when violence seems to reign, and for a path to Divinity when all seems lost. And as always, the Angels respond, hastening to our side to help us find the path.

Chapter 7 - What Exactly Are Angels?

The Traditional Scoop

When we speak of angels, we speak of a group within a group. That is, the word 'angel' names a spiritual being who functions as a messenger of divinity; at the same time, among the beings we call angels are groups of beings, one group of which is also called 'angel.' The groups are called choirs, and there are nine choirs of angels.

The idea of ordering angels is credited to the writings of someone scholars refer to as Pseudo-Dionysius. At the time he wrote, around the 5th or 6th C CE, it was a common practice for writers to pen their works under not their own names but under the name of another, more famous person. They saw this as a way of honouring these famous people, as well as a way to get a larger audience for the works.

His writings, concerning Christian mysticism, were presented as the work of Dionysius the Aeropagite. Dionysius was a convert of St. Paul, so obviously he was long dead by the time Pseudo-Dionysius wrote. The real author is thought to have been a Syrian priest, and his work shows a strong neoplatonic influence.

The element we are concerned with is his division and ordering of the angelic realm. He modeled it after the platonic patterns using the number three, which was regarded as a mystical number. Since his work was published, his order of angels has been accepted by theologians and those who study angels. It is by no means the only ordering system of the angelic ranks, but it is the most widely accepted.

Pseudo-Dionysius saw the world in a hierarchical fashion. God's power, as well as God's love, came to earth not directly from God to world. Instead, it was 'stepped' through many levels. This stepping-type transference of God's loving power is accomplished by the angels in bucket-brigade style...think of Jacob's dream - the angels ascending and descending to heaven.

In Pseudo-Dionysius's understanding, humans were at the bottom of the chain, with God at the top. The angels form the 'steps' of a ladder-like progression of spiritual perfection. Humans, as well as the lower angelic ranks, are assisted by those above to grow spiritually, thus rising higher.

In addition, the upper ranks, including God, are able to relate to humans - who cannot perceive the perfection of the higher levels- through the assistance of the intermediate levels of angel.

The angelic hierarchy Pseudo-Dionysius created is in the form of a triple trio - three groups of three. The groupings are based on the Old Testament orders of angels and also on the writings of St. Paul.

The highest level of angels is composed of the Seraphim, Cherubim, and Thrones. These angels see and adore God directly, being in direct contact with God. They are viewed as the purest angels and those having greatest wisdom and power. It is their joy to sing praise to God at every moment.

The highest order of angels are the Seraphim, which means "the burning ones." These angels possess an intense ardor for God. They see God most clearly, standing as guardians before the throne of God. The book of Isaiah tells us that they offer constant praise to God, singing "Holy, Holy, Holy is the Lord of Hosts." They are described as having six wings – two for flying, and two each to cover their faces and feet.

Next come the Cherubim, meaning "The ones with knowledge," who are communicators of the Divine Will. These angels are said to contemplate God's providence and plan for creation. They are also regarded as the angels who serve as guards of sacred places.

It is cherubim who guard the gate to Eden in Genesis and who protect the Ark of the Covenant in Exodus. They guard the stars, as well, and bring enlightenment to the angels below them. Like Seraphim, they praise God continually.

Finally, the Thrones are angels of humility and peace. Ezekiel describes them as wheel-like beings with many eyes. They bear God through the universe where material creation is formed. As they have the task of contemplating and upholding divine will and justice, they are characterized by their humble submission to God's good will.

The next Choir of angels serve to govern the heavens and to fulfill divine providence for the universe. They both imitate and serve God.

The first order in this choir are the Dominions, who make known God's commands to humans and angels. They govern the lesser choirs of angels and channel the majesty and mercy of God. They influence earthy governments, as well, inspiring them to godly oversight.

The second order are the Virtues, also known as the Authorities. They are the 'Shining Ones' who carry out the directions of God and control the elements. They regulate seasons and heavenly bodies and all of nature. They show the meaning of divine authority in the administration of miracles.

The third group are the Powers, and they are indeed powerful angels. They are the celestial enforcers who fight evil spirits as warriors. These angels have boundless courage as they battle the dark forces. Perhaps because of their interaction with darkness, Paul had reservations about this choir; nevertheless, they are accepted as important angels within the nine orders. (Romans 8:37–39)

The final choir consists of angels who work with humans. They bring God's will and purpose, guiding humans and assisting them in daily life.

The Principalities are the first order on this level. Along with the Powers, their goodness is questioned by St. Paul, but they are nevertheless regarded as holy and powerful angels. Their task is to protect the nations. In that effort, they guard national leaders and work to inspire policies that uphold the holy will and justice of God.

The next order is the Archangels, the chief angels, who bring important messages from God to people. Three archangels are named in the Christian scriptures - Michael, Gabriel, and Raphael. Others, named in early church documents and in holy books such as the Kabbalah, include Uriel, Chamuel, Jophiel, and Zadkiel. The Archangels watch and assist the Angels in their holy tasks.

Finally are the Angels who are closest to people and who guard and help us in our lives, particularly in matters involving spiritual progress and growth. They are the true messengers, taking our prayers up to heaven and bringing answers to us. Especially, they serve as guardians to humans.

This vision of angelic organization has been used by the Christian churches since around the 4-6th Centuries.

Today, the distinctions between orders of angels is not as important an understanding as in Pseudo-Dionysius's day. Perhaps this is due to a general acceptance of the idea that people can communicate directly with divinity without the agency of angels.

Part 2

How to Communicate with Your Angels

As we move into this important part of the book, let us begin by saying that ours is not the only way of understanding Angels. In our practice and our work with our heavenly friends, this is what we have come to understand with their guidance. Truth is truth on many levels, so please take what resonates and leave the rest.

Over the past fifteen years we have helped hundreds of people connect with their angels and receive guidance and assistance. In this part of the book, you will meet your angels and begin a deeper relationship with them.

Journaling is especially important in this section. There are also many activities to help you develop your "angel ears" and hear their voices and discern their presence with you.

Chapter 8 – How We Have Come to Understand Angels

In our conversations with Angels, we have discovered that the angelic realm has no real divisions or actual hierarchy. Every angel has a purpose and a special quality and like the strings on a guitar, they are in harmony with one another and work together as necessary. As one works, all the "strings" resonate.

One of our angels, Mickey, has helped us understand the roles of angels by describing the spirit world as a "cookie". He says that there are many ingredients that go in to making a cookie: flour, shortening, sugar, eggs, chips, vanilla etc., all distinct elements that have their own qualities and purpose.

When they are mixed together, all those separate components are blended to make the cookie. All the ingredients are in it. You can see a chocolate chip in the mixture. You can taste the vanilla. You know that the cookie is made up of all kinds of parts that work together to create something good, but you would not be correct to think you have an egg or a cup of shortening or a chocolate chip. You have a cookie, and all these elements that are present have combined to create something different from any one of them.

So too, with Angels. They are all components of the big whole and all streaming from the same source - our loving Creator. Call on one angel for a specific task and that angel comes forward supported by the unity and love of the combined whole.

Guardian Angels

It is generally understood that everyone has at least one guardian angel. This is the angel who is with you at your birth and will accompany you throughout your life - and even beyond. Deb received a teaching that the Guardian Angel is a soul companion, journeying with us through eternity and lifetimes. Who would know us better?

There are other angels who come to assist for varying lengths of time as you have need. For example, those going through health challenges have angels to help in the healing process. Those who are in high risk jobs tend to have a larger entourage to guide and assist in their work. If you are doing a special project, you probably have an angel to lend support.

Teachers, healers, and those who do spiritual work generally have quite a few angels on hand for assistance. The more potential your work has for touching people on deep levels, the more angelic assistance and support is yours.

We have many angels that help us with various aspects of our work. For example, Deb is assisted by angels when she officiates at weddings, and more when she meets with grieving families planning a funeral. With angels who help us with our work to angels that help us when we write and more angels when we counsel, it can get a little crowded here, spiritually speaking.

Remember that every created thing has an angel, according to St. Thomas Aquinas, so your home has an angel, you place of work has an angel, your car has an angel– you are literally surrounded by angels wherever you go. Once you begin to perceive this on an intuitive level, you can really get the angelic world working with you!

The Archangels
We thought it was important to include a section about the Archangels. In popular angel work, many practitioners and readers refer to them and their perceived "powers." Angels are certainly

powerful, but they never act independently - only under Divine will.

A misconception around the Archangels is that they are somehow better or higher or more powerful than garden-variety Angels, if such a thing could be. Sometimes people who work with Angels boast that they work with only Archangels or that they work with
Archangel Michael, etc.

The more we work with Angels, the more we have come to understand what it is to be without ego. We are given to understand that the titles we ascribe to Angels do not indicate reality from their perspective at all. Originally, there were considered to be two kinds of Angels - Archangels and Angels, with archangels being the leaders. The choirs - as outlined in Part I- with their hierarchy is useful only in terms of categorizing areas in which angels may serve.

From them, we are told that it is more accurate to say, 'They serve' and leave it at that, for their nature is love and their activity is service. How and when and whom they serve is simply a matter of need.

That being said, we humans are most comfortable with labels and names and therefore we classify Angels and so there are those called Archangels.

First, who are they? In the Judaic tradition, including the Kabbalah, there are many Archangels listed. They include Michael, Raphael, Gabriel, Uriel, Sariel, Raguel, Remiel, Zadkiel, Jophiel, Haniel, and Chamuel. The Islamic tradition names Michael/ Mikael, Gabriel/Jibril, Azrael, Israfil/Isra'afeel, Malik, Munkar, and Nakir.

In the western Christian tradition, three Archangels are named: Michael, Raphael, and Gabriel. The Eastern Orthodox church venerates the Seven Holy Archangels - the three mentioned plus

Uriel, Selaphiel, Jegudiel, and Barachiel. Pope Zachary, in 745 A.D., took the names of seven Angels from the list of those accepted by the Church; those removed included Uriel and Raguel, who appear above.

The Zoroastrian tradition does not name spiritual beings as angels and archangels. Instead these spirits are called the 'Amesha Spenta' or Bountiful Immortals. There are six which would correspond to Archangels in the Western traditions. They have names like Vohu Manu and Kshathra Vairya and rule over specific aspects of creation such as animal life and metals and minerals, respectively.

According to the hierarchical choir developed by Pseudo-Dionysius, Archangels stand at the throne of God and bring messages to people from God. They are said to direct heaven's 'army' in the 'war' of good and evil. Archangels are said to oversee guardian angels in the protection of humans and may themselves serve as guardians of people with very important, far-reaching tasks. Archangels serve the Will of God directly in relation to humans, bringing strength and comfort by means of Divine unconditional love.

It's easy to see where people got the idea of Archangels being higher or better than plain-angels. And it is easy to see the idea that working with an Archangel is somehow superior to working with an 'ordinary' angel following from this.

But no. Archangels are happy to help all of us and, being outside the time and space constraints of life on earth, are easily able to help all of us at the same time, if necessary. Working with Archangels, or seeking their help, is more an indication of our perception of the need than it is an indicator of our goodness, skill, or power.

Archangels willingly offer guidance and help people find their next step in life or their divine mission. When asked for assistance, they gladly bring insights and understanding to bear on the issue. They help us become more sympathetic and generous as we strive to become ever more perfect channels of love. They help us to understand that all things work for good, if we but let them, and guide us to transform negativity in our lives.

We are given to understand that when we call for help, the most appropriate Angel takes the call, so to speak. Whether 'appropriate' refers to being free to assist, a la the old British sitcom "Are You Being Served?" or being an energetic match, or simply being a response to a call for that specific Angel - we are always helped by the best Angel for the task.

Nevertheless, the Archangels are considered in angel lore to have special tasks and areas of responsibilities. With that in mind, then, it may be more appealing to request particular Angels for particular needs.

Archangel Michael

Michael means 'Who is like God.' Michael is sometimes referred to as The Prince of Light. He is depicted as a large angel holding a sword. Michael is considered the Warrior Angel, the protector of Heaven. Michael is regarded as the heavenly counterpart of Jesus among Jehovah's Witnesses, and the Urantia book makes a similar association.

The Book of Revelation, in the Christian scriptures, speaks of Archangel Michael as the angel who defeated Satan in Heaven. For this reason, Michael has come to be sought in situations involving safety or requiring courage. For example, when one is in a dangerous part of town, Michael might be asked for protection.

Wherever there is conflict, whether between nations or within homes, Michael is traditionally the Angel whose assistance is needed, especially if there is an issue of objective good involved. Situations of injustice or cases in which power is being abused to victimize helpless others would be examples, as would instances of disharmony, such as a family conflict.

Among those who call themselves Lightworkers, referring to their spiritual efforts with regard to ascension, Michael is seen as a patron of sorts. They see Michael's protective role extending to the energies with which they work. When there are issues of negativity, lightworkers seek Michael's aid to release negative energies from places or objects as well as from people's hearts and minds.

In working with Archangel Michael, seek to grow in those qualities associated with him: fearless pursuit of right, courage in facing evil, strength in protecting the weak or helpless. Ask Michael's help to remain grounded in goodness and light and to resist temptations to darkness and despair.

Because so many ideas coming from mass/cultural consciousness are grounded in fear, judgement, and condemnation, Michael's help can be invaluable in transforming our societies into more loving communities.

Over the centuries and now, among New Age devotees and occultists, Michael has become associated with the South, fire, summer, and the colour red. Because of his devotion to right and Light, Michael is often invoked in matters of involving career, work, and life purpose.

Archangel Gabriel

The name Gabriel means 'God is my strength.' Gabriel is referred to as the messenger Angel and is often shown with a lily or trumpet. Sometimes Gabriel is pictured holding a spear or shield. Gabriel is the Angel who, in the Christian nativity story, visited Zachary to announce the upcoming birth of John the Baptist, later visiting the Blessed Virgin Mary to tell her that she would become the mother of Jesus.

In the Jewish testament, Gabriel gives Daniel messages and insights, while in the Talmud, he is shown as the destroyer of Sennacherib's armies. In Islamic tradition, Gabriel is thought to have given the Koran to Mohammad.

Because of Gabriel's traditional role, he is considered a patron of those whose lifework involves communication, such as teachers, writers, broadcasters, etc.

Whenever there are problems arising from poor communication, whenever one must speak clearly and well or present an idea of viewpoint to others, Gabriel is the angel to call. If one is planning to ask for a favour, a salary increase, or a loan - Gabriel can help.

In addition to situations involving clear communication, Gabriel's aid is invoked in issues around childbirth, due to this Angel's role in the birth of Jesus. This Angel is often asked to assist when a pregnancy is desired. In related situations - such as when a childbirth is in jeopardy or an easy delivery is sought - this angel is quick to help.

Other forms of creativity aside from childbirth are also within Gabriel's range of influence. If one feels blocked in painting, writing, or other form of creative expression, call on Gabriel.

Gabriel's associations include the Western direction, water, autumn, and blue. Gabriel is invoked in issues around messages, communication, and creation. He is patron of postal workers, journalists and broadcasters, and those who assist in the delivery of messages and communications of all kinds.

Archangel Raphael

Raphael means "God has healed" or "God Heals." This Archangel is the Angel of healing in every form and body (mental, physical, emotional, spiritual). Raphael is also considered the healer of the Earth itself.

Raphael appears in the apocryphal book of Tobit, one of the books Catholics accept as part of the Christian New Testament. In that book is found the story of Tobias, whose son was accompanied by this angel (under the guise of a man) on a journey. When they return to Tobias, Raphael heals his blindness and identifies himself as "the angel Raphael, one of the seven, who stand before the Lord" (Tobit, xii, 15).

It is Raphael, followers of Islam believe, who will blow the trumpet or Soor that announces the Day of Judgement.

Raphael is associated with the East, the element of air, springtime, and the colour yellow or green.

Whenever there is pain of any kind, Raphael is the Angel to call for help. For that reason, he is the patron to doctors and nurses, and all therapists. In addition, Raphael is seen as the Angel of science and knowledge and so is patron to researchers and scientists, particularly those whose research affects healing and wellness.

When invoked in matters of healing, Raphael's help may take many forms. There may, of course, be a miracle of healing and recovery. Caregivers may be guided as to treatments and insights that support the recovery of the patient. Procedures may be developed that offer relief.

In addition, Raphael works through healing of memories and past issues. Guidance given may include nutritional and psychological direction.

Finally, in consideration of Raphael's protection of young Tobias on his journey, Raphael is also the patron of travelers. Invite him on every trip, asking him to keep you safe, the gas tank filled, the vehicle operating smoothly, and the traffic moving freely.

Archangel Uriel
Of the major Archangels, Uriel is the least familiar in the West. Uriel means "Flame of God" or "Light of God."

Uriel does not appear in the Christian scriptures; the book of Enoch, in speaking of this Archangel calls him, "one of the holy angels, who is over the world... the leader of them all." In Jewish mystical tradition, Uriel is the Angel of Sunday, of Poetry, and one of the holy Sephiroth. It is Uriel who is believed to have wrestled

Jacob and to have told Noah about the upcoming Great Flood. Uriel checked the doors of Egypt for lamb's blood during the plague and, during the End Times, is the keeper of the key to the Pit.

As the light of God, Uriel brings understanding when called for assistance. Uriel is able to show us the divine vision of our lives. When we suffer pain and disappointment, Uriel will reveal to us the blessings and lessons contained within them.

Perhaps the most significant 'light' Uriel brings to us is an understanding of the importance of forgiveness. When there is discord or anger, Uriel can bring light to bear on the matter so that we see the harm such anger and resentment does to our spirits and bodies. As the Flame of God, Uriel seeks to kindle in us the flame of divine love. It is this love that allows us to move past anger into forgiveness and find peace once more.

In any situation requiring light - emotional and mental understanding as well as information to restore harmony, peace, or right action - Uriel can bring his gift of wisdom and love to bear.

Uriel is often painted holding a book to represent his wisdom. He is considered the angel patron of art, music, and poetry. In later years, Uriel has come to be the patron of ecology as well and is often called the Angel of the Earth. Uriel is correctly asked to intercede in matters concerning the wellbeing and protection of the planet.

The associations for Uriel include the colour black (and sometimes green), the direction North, the element of earth, and the season of winter.

Chapter 9 - Satan and the Dark Angels

At every workshop or group we lead, questions about dark angels always arise. We are of the belief that these negative energies are much more interested in bigger kinds of circumstances and situations than interfering with individual human lives. We have all powerful, God-given Guardian Angels to deal with them, so we do not give them much thought.

But the question is on a lot of people's minds and apparently, it has been for a very long time. It seems that as soon as humans acknowledged a deity, they also recognized an anti-god as well.

In Zoroastrianism, the ancient faith which influenced all major religions, God or Ahura Mazda is opposed by an evil spirit, Angra Mainyu, whose power is equal or nearly so to his own.

Judaism, on the other hand, recognized a supreme being. Yahweh was the creator of all that is, including evil spirits. In fact, Satan– more properly called the Satan, meaning an adversary– began as a good angel who fell from grace.

The Satan appears in the Old Testament story of Balaam, a magician who opposed God's will. There, the Satan prevents Balaam from committing evil, which seems to be a real switch of sides unless one realizes that the Satan was unable to act independently of God. When the Satan turns his attention to Job, for example, he acted only with the permission and will of God.

The Satan, therefore wasn't seen as a completely evil being. For that, the Jews of the Hebrew Scriptures turned to the beasts such as Leviathan and Behemoth, the serpent and the dragon. We see this in Genesis when the serpent convinces Eve to disobey God's instructions.

It is only later in history, in later versions of scripture, that the serpent and other evil spirits become synonymous with the Prince of Darkness or Satan.

Fallen angels are another story. These fallen angels are seen as serving Satan and seeking the fall of humans. Why did they fall? The most accepted reasons are lust, pride, and disobedience to God.

Origen, one of the fathers of the Early Church, taught that the angels had free will, as humans did. In the exercise of their free will, some angels drifted farther from God. In Origen's view, as angels drifted farther and farther away, the angelic hierarchy was created. Angels, being in the lowest level in the hierarchy, who drifted farther became human.

Those who moved even farther from God became demons, the inhabitants of Hell. Not surprisingly, this is not a widely-taught or accepted view, but one that reveals the challenge humankind faces when trying to explain the bad influences in the world.

In the Book of Enoch, found in the Pseudepigrapha of the Old Testament, there is a story about angels sent to Earth to create Eden. These 'watchers' fell in love with human women and took wives among them, giving rise to a race of giants called the Nephilim. This angered God, causing him to cast them from Heaven, make them mortal, and transform them to demons. This story is alluded to in the Book of Genesis.

Many Christians have heard the story of Lucifer, the brightest and most powerful angel in heaven. In that story, Lucifer was second only to God in beauty, intelligence, brilliance and power. Growing ambitious, Lucifer decided to make himself equal to God. At this, Lucifer was cast from Heaven. This story is similar to those in some Canaanite stories of their own gods.

The existence of the fallen angels was also explained in several stories not included in the Old Testament. One of the most interesting is found in the Life of Adam and Eve. In this apocryphal book, the first humans were created by God and placed above the angels, who were commanded to bow to these mortals.

The Satan stubbornly resisted, insisting that his creation before that of humans entitled him to their worship instead. For this disobedience, the Satan was expelled from the heavenly realm.

Iblis, the Satan's Islamic counterpart, met a similar situation and fate. In the Moslem version of the story, Iblis incites a heavenly rebellion rather than worship the humans. After his expulsion, like the serpent in Genesis, he encourages the humans to disregard God's commands to them.

Occasionally, Iblis is shown as loving God far too much to worship a lowly human being. Whatever the reason, however, the outcome is the same: he refuses to bow to Adam and is cast out.

These stories are particularly interesting when one considers the relationship between Jesus and Adam. In Eden, Adam gave humans a legacy of sin, pain, and death. As the new Adam, Jesus brought humans from sin into life with his legacy of redemption, renewal, and resurrection. The "new Adam," Jesus the God-man, receives the adoration of the angels and is elevated far above both the good and fallen angels, who cannot fail to praise his name.

If the early stories are true, the fallen angels are supremely trumped by the mystery of the Incarnation.

If the Christian scripture is filled with references to angels, it is filled as well with references to their evil brethren, the devils. Jesus is tempted by and battles Satan in the wilderness. Being confronted by his enemies, he tells them that they have been fathered by the devil, who is a liar and the father of lies.

Throughout his ministry on earth, Jesus freed people, whether they were possessed by demons or simply living in darkness. Jesus cast out devils wherever he went.

The existence of evil is explained in the Book of Revelation, also. In chapter 12, Michael and the good angels fight against the dragon, ultimately casting him from heaven. This dragon is identified as the Devil and Satan, the deceiver of the whole world. And it is not hell to which he is cast in this chapter but earth, where we are told he went off to make war on those who keep the commandments of God and hold the testimony of Jesus.

What a frightening idea to the new Christians, that they were the target of the dragon, Satan! It is not surprising, therefore, that Paul in his epistles refers often to Satan and the devils who follow him. He exhorts the faithful to be vigilant against this enemy, to put on the whole armor of God that they may stand against the wiles of the devil, even as he reminds them that Christ by his death has taken away the devil's power.

Paul seems to spot Satan everywhere, advising the community of believers that Satan may disguise himself as an angel of light.

In that vein, therefore, he urges them to ignore any preaching different from what they have been heard, even if it be from an angel. Or a devil masquerading as an angel, we would say.

Despite their tradition of holy angels who defend the people of God, the Christians would have heard Paul's words with some dismay. Were their angel guardians strong enough to protect them from the powers of the evil spirits? In answer, the holy psalmist proclaimed, "The angel of the Lord encamps around those who fear him and delivers them." (Psalm 34, verse 7).

In the beautiful and consoling Psalm 91, the writer praises God for the care and protection given his faithful: "For he will command his angels concerning you to guard you in all your ways. On their hands they will bear you up, so that you will not dash your foot against a stone."

Even the Apostles must have been concerned about the dragon and fearful of his power. In joy and awe, they observed their

Master as he ministered to people possessed by demons, casting them forth and freeing their victims. When he sent out the seventy following the Transfiguration, he commanded them to go out as laborers into his harvest, curing the sick and proclaiming in every town they visited that the kingdom of God had come.

Still, it must have been with some trepidation that they obeyed the Lord, as on their return they exclaimed with surprise, "Lord, in your name even the demons submit to us!" Jesus's reply comforts both them and us: "I watched Satan fall from heaven like a flash of lightning. See, I have given you authority to tread on snakes and scorpions, and over all the power of the enemy; and nothing will hurt you." (Luke 10:18-19.)

James the brother of Jesus dismisses our fears with an unconcern borne of great faith and trust. "Resist the devil, and he will flee from you. Draw near to God, and he will draw near to you," he counsels his followers.

Even today, so many years later, the idea of fallen angels continues to disturb faithful men and women who fear that they may be led astray by the deceit of the evil one. They wonder whether our angel guardians truly powerful enough to protect us against such demonic forces.

The remedy given to the early church is given to us as well: our will to resist the devil, the authority Christ says is ours, and our powerful guardian angel ever at our side. With these, we need not fear.

Chapter 10 - Discerning Angels

"But," you may ask, "How CAN I be more aware of the angels in my life and around me every day? How can I be sure that I am hearing their direction? How do I even know it IS an angel? How do angels work with us, anyway?"

These are questions we hear in every angel workshop we conduct, and they are excellent, important questions. Angels are far more intelligent than the most brilliant human being. They find all kinds of ways to work with us throughout each day.

Even those who haven't got a clue that there are such things as angels are still receiving the benefit of angelic protection, guidance and assistance. You don't have to hear your angel, but it sure helps things along.

We humans are very finite beings, grounded in the mundane physical world. We tend to believe what we see and to mistrust our hunches or "gut feelings." We value common sense – but what is that really? Often, it is really someone else's vision way of what makes logical sense or, more importantly, what society thinks OUGHT to make sense to us.

Being earthbound means that we rely on our five physical senses -- touch, taste, smell, sight and hearing – to give us information about the world around us. Our senses are the channels through which we come to understand what we are, what the world contains, how the world works.

In primitive times, information perceived through the senses meant the difference between life and death. Today, we rely less on our sense of smell, for example, to alert us to danger - and the danger in question is not likely to be a wild animal but perhaps a gas leak. Still, our very cells are programmed by thousands of years of human development to depend on our physical senses for the information we need to live a successful life.

Our physical ego self has a vested interest in keeping our attention on the here and now, on what is tangible and real. This, our physical ego self tells us, is what is true. Everything else is airy-fairy wishful thinking. It's fantastical illusions that may be fun to think about, but when you're down to the wire, it's action and savvy that count - not pretty ideas that can't be proven.

Working with the spiritual realm runs directly counter to an instinct that tells us to trust only what we can see, hear, or touch. Our spiritual insights tell us that the unseen world is more vibrant and alive than the one we view each morning, but accepting it isn't easy.

Seen, unseen. Spiritual self, physical ego self. It's quite a balancing act, so we can be forgiven if we don't always manage to keep as spiritually open as we wish.

Angels understand this. Unless they are working with those who are more open to intuitive and spiritual understandings, it can be difficult for them to get our attention and even harder to get a message through in a clear, understandable fashion. They must get past our conscious, physical mind to get through to us, and they do this in many ways.

How Angels Come to Us

Dreams and Visions

The first way angels come to us is in our dreams and visions. We hear about this occurring in many stories of the old and new testaments of the Bible. It's easier for them to come to us when our physical, ego selves are down for the count; they can work with the images of our dreamscapes to communicate directly to our unconscious minds.

Later in the day, or perhaps days later, a dream image that refuses to be dismissed may be the very prompting you need to go to a particular park - where you meet someone who becomes very important to you. Or an unsettling dream may be the catalyst to drive you to a reader or spiritual teacher who proves to have information that changes your life.

Teachings can also be given in our dreams. We may not recall them upon awakening, but we can trust them to come to our consciousness when they are needed. It may be that a situation that has puzzled us now makes sense for no good reason, or we may offer the perfect answer to someone's problem without knowing the source of that flash of insight. Often, dream insights surface in such ways.

Angels often come in our dreams to bring us comfort and support. They may accompany loved ones who have crossed over, and we awaken recalling that we dreamed of Mama, and what a lovely visit we had. We believe that those visits are real indeed, orchestrated through our angels.

Sometimes we have dreams that simply bring us peace or the

sense of such love and joy. Often, we are told, those dreams reflect time spent in heavenly company.

As you continue your work, you may find that your dreams become more vivid. You may find yourself dreaming of an angel or another wise figure and awaken with the feeling that something significant occurred in the dream.

We encourage you to keep a notepad on your bedside table to record whatever dream fragments remain; as you continue the practice, you will remember more and more information from your dreams.

When you show faithful commitment to this practice, your dreams will then become channels your angels can use to communicate with you.

Who was that Person?
The second way that angels can come to us is as other people: strangers who enter our lives in moments of crisis and leave just as quickly when things are resolved, leaving us scratching our heads. They come in moments of great need and by invitation.

Deb has a great story of an encounter she had in a grocery store bright and early one morning. She was stressed and in a rush and was met with this lovely fellow with a huge grin who smiled at her and said good morning. She said good morning and rushed to pick up her items.

It seemed that everywhere she went, she ran into the man with the big smile. And finally, at the check-out, there he was cracking jokes and laughing. At one point he turned to Deb and made a comment that things have a way of working out and to stay in her joy –strange indeed from someone who didn't know the current events of her life.

She happened to glance at his shirt –it was a uniform shirt with his name on it: "Godson." Then she had a feeling of recognition. Interesting name... she looked at the fellow and realized he was glowing with happiness. His good mood was infectious as all the sleepy people in line began to loosen up and laugh along with him.

Was he an angel? He could have simply been responding to guidance he didn't know he was receiving from his angel. Perhaps angels were shining through him to bring joy wherever he went. Whoever he was, he had a positive impact on Deb's day and lightened her mood considerably. This is a hallmark of angelic involvement.

Angels come to us as male or female. They may drive off in a car or they may simply be...gone without a trace. They may be strangers acting under inspiration or even a loved one who gives us just the information we need, surprising themselves that they ever thought of it. One thing is for certain –we cannot force an angel to appear to us, but they are quite adept at taking form when it is important.

You might find that as you become sensitive to angelic energies, you may discern that some angels seem to have have more masculine energy and some have more feminine qualities. This is not an indication that an angel is male or female. Angels have no gender, but we may perceive them as more like one gender or the other. This is simply our human interpretation of the qualities we associate with being manly or womanly.

Animal Angels

Angels can occasionally manifest to us as animals. We hear lots of protection stories in which humans were kept safe by dogs, wolves, and even horses. Animals often figure prominently in stories of enlightenment and understanding. Birds often convey messages of comfort and even life after death.

Some years ago in Toronto, a distraught man drove to a city park. In his car he had five guns, including rifles and a semi-automatic weapon. He had 6000 rounds of ammunition and a plan: he was going to kill all the people in the park, then drive around killing people until he was apprehended and sentenced to life in prison.

He'd actually loaded his pistols and, standing at the trunk of his car, had begun getting ready for the rampage by taking the guns off the safety and the trigger locks. A dog came bounding from the park, tongue hanging out, smiling as dogs do.

The man didn't want to play, but the dog was insistent on making friends with him. Before his desperation had set in, the man had been a pet lover himself, and as the dog tried to entice him, he rethought his plan. He turned himself in to police. No guns were fired, no one was hurt.

We've been asked whether that dog was an angel. Did they use that friendly dog to accomplish their task of saving the people there whom they guarded? We can never know with certainty. However, although we don't know, but it certainly seems to us that angels were there that afternoon to accomplish heaven's purpose. (*Dog Ends Gunman's Plan for Shooting Rampage*, Joe Friesen, Toronto Globe and Mail, Published June 24, 2004)

As you work more closely with your Angels, you may find yourself noticing animals and responding differently from before. You might find yourself being aware of messages being conveyed by animals around you. If you have not been much concerned with ecology or climate change, you might notice growing awareness of such issues and perhaps growing upset at the thought of, say, glaciers melting.

If that happens, don't be alarmed. Remember that Angels are charged with the workings of creation. It may be that you are being called to deeper love of the planet and its creatures.

Chapter 11 - How Angels Communicate with Us

Remember when you read that we humans learned about the world through our five senses? This is natural, for our ego-based personalities are part of our physical make-up as humans.

The spiritual world, though, is often called the "supernatural" world because it is not ordinarily perceivable through our physical senses. Because we learn to perceive the world around us though those physical senses, it can be difficult for us to become aware of the spiritual world in which we live and move.

For that reason, angels often come to us in dreams, when our ego-personalities are at rest and not resistant to angelic interaction. Our angels are not only interested in working with us as we sleep, though. They have insights and guidance to help us through our waking day.

But before they can share those messages, they have to get our attention.

Often, angels use physical cues such as chills, goosebumps, tingling, unusual clarity of vision, a fragrance or sounds such as ringing or tones to get through to us. These may draw our attention to something or someone important.

Many people report such phenomena upon meeting a significant person for the first time. They may say that everything else seemed to disappear, leaving the two of them alone in a cocoon of warmth. Or they might remember tingles as they were introduced.

Students have told us of being unable to find a memento of a recently departed loved one. Then, they tell us, they found it where they had already looked carefully, where it could not logically have been, only – there it was.

One reported needing important information and being unable to access it. Later, when she was given a book she'd never seen before -- which was later discovered to have exactly the information she needed – she felt a kind of 'thud' in her midsection. Some report getting teary, others feeling weak or dizzy when such a 'coincidence' occurs.

The oddity and the inexplicable quality of such physical sensations alert us that something of importance has occurred, whether we understand its significance or not. Such phenomena are often dismissed by our rational mind, leaving us feeling confused - unless we recognize what has happened as an angelic intervention.

Another way that angels connect with us is through Synchronicity. This is a Jungian term that talks about unusual things coinciding at the same time. For example, Deb might mention a song she enjoyed years ago and wishing she had a recording of it, only to hear it the very next day. Once, we might have thought to ourselves, "That's weird." Now we just say, "Angels…"

Perhaps a word, image, idea, or song that you awaken remembering is an angel's communication to you. It may be an event or moment of insight. It may come in a phone call, or a sentence from the morning paper, or a bit of conversation overheard. However it comes, it nags at you. When that happens, pay attention. Remember that the alert will attract your notice. You may be tempted to call it a coincidence.

Recognize that the answer to a question you have asked may come in more usual ways: insights, inspirations, conversations, flashes, coincidences, etc. You may hear songs on radio, experience chance meetings, or catch bits of unexpected conversations, any of which may bring an unexpected understanding.

You might find yourself thinking of a person you'd like to speak with -- and then phone rings, and you hear that very person's hello.

Angels often use our thoughts, emotions, and memories to communicate with us. When thoughts come unbidden and will not leave us alone, when seemingly irrelevant memories command our attention, when we feel sudden bursts of joy or peace or other loving emotion - it may be angels at work. It's worth it to take a minute to check within to see whether there is a message within the event and what that message is.

Angels can also use visual cues to bring you to awareness of their presence. Be aware of images, colours and pictures that may draw your attention.

Angels are constantly working to inspire us and help us in our day. As we consider choices, concerns, or challenges, try to be aware of any memories that may bubble up and offer insight to the situation. You may receive ideas or new insights. We find that when we get an idea that is angelically inspired, it tends to come as a whole package.

Rather than just a thread of an idea that seems vague, an angelic inspiration is global with a clarity around beginning, middle and end; it doesn't require the step-by-step 'fleshing out' that human ideas need.

Don't worry if you miss the message first time around, they will keep working to get your attention! Deb remembers an incident that happened during another very difficult time of her life. She and Jean were driving and talking about the situation.

They passed a billboard for a jazz radio station and suddenly, Jean was moved to change the dial on Deb's car radio – something she had never done before and actually regarded as quite rude!

As the very next song began, Deborah gasped. The day before she had been humming this beloved but obscure tune, trying to remember the chorus. She hadn't heard it in 20 years and she knew it was important but could remember the lyrics.

Guess which song had begun playing when Jean changed the radio station? The song she hadn't heard in two decades! And the chorus brought her to tears: "And the riverbank talks of the waters of March; it's the end of all strain, it's the joy in your heart." Angels in action!

Not only will angels continue working to get your attention, they never compel you. Always, you have free will, so you are free to follow through with inspired action or to pass. And if you want to pass, that's ok: the angels will find another person to complete the work, so there's no guilt for your choice.

When we work with angels, we can be sure they will never condemn or judge us. They bring us assurance and support as we move through our day. As questions or concerns arise, we can ask our angels for their guidance. Their responses are marked by outpouring of love, acceptance, self-love, self-understanding, inner peace, being deeply cared for, or other positive emotions – even when we reject their leadings.

Angels most usually use one or a combination of these means to connect with us. Lets take a look at the many ways that we can communicate with them.

Chapter 12 - Ways to Interact with Angels

You can use many ways to work with your angels. As you get more comfortable with the back and forth dialogue, you will find that you can simply carry on a conversation with your Angel mentally. As you open to your Angel's guidance voice, you'll find the way that works best for you.

Here are several very effective methods to communicate with your angels. You don't have to try them all immediately. Choose one technique to explore, then try others to find the ones that work best for you.

Angel Letters: The Angelic Post Office
This is a powerful exercise and a great way to release the things that challenge you. You'll need a notebook or journal.

Ground and relax. Take several deep breaths and breath evenly and comfortably. Turn your attention inward and focus on your angel.

Think of your angel and feel its gentle energy. Date the letter and begin, writing, "Dear Angel" or use its name, if you have one. Let the words flow, writing as you would to a very close friend. You can ask advice or guidance. Finally, say thanks and then sign it.

Put your letter in a special box, under your pillow, in your Bible, etc. You can bury or burn it, if that seems more satisfactory to you. You'll know what to do with it.

However you handle the letter, send it off in peace. You can be sure that your angel, on receiving the words of your heart, will now act for your highest and best.

Another way of using this means of calling angels to your aid is simply to list the need and call the type of angel who can best handle it.

"Dear Angels of Communication, please intercede in my dealings with my nasty neighbour to bring a peaceful resolution to the matter at hand." "Dear Angels of Healing, please give my doctor insight into what is making me ill. Inspire him to the perfect treatment to obtain my return to radiant health."

Think of the need you are presenting, then direct your request accordingly. Many people have found this an effective means of quick answers to their need.

You may wonder, "How do I know it is my Angel and not my own thoughts?"

This is the $64,000 question, isn't it? It is an important question for us all and, even after many many years of daily angel journaling, we still sometimes wonder if we aren't just getting our own ideas instead of an angelic answer. But we aren't, and you will learn when you aren't, either.

Here is an exercise to help you see the difference between your words and the angels' words.

IMPORTANT: Stop right now and do this next exercise before going on.

Conscious Creation Exercise:
1. Take a moment and think of your favorite recipe. Write a list of ingredients that you need to get from the grocery store.

2. You are having a party! Write directions to your house for your guests.

3. Compose a six-line poem about the return of Spring or your fa-

vorite season of the year.

Did you notice that as you wrote you had to stop and think about each task?

Your pen probably stopped and started as you expressed the thought. You may have gone blank a few times as you had to re-call the ingredients for the recipe or the name of a street near your home. Perhaps you found it necessary to go back and fill in details you forgot. Some things came quickly but there was thought, or-ganizing, and a deliberate conscious effort to write things down.

This is the experience of putting your own ideas to paper: think-ing, writing, making changes and corrections, and so on.

The Angel Journal...
Conversations with Angels.

If you haven't been working with your angels, this is the most effective method that we have found to get direct guidance from them. It takes some practise, but it is well worth the effort.

What is angel writing?
Angel writing is a way to get clear guidance from our angels and provides a quick method to have a dialogue. It is one of the most immediate and effective ways to receive insights and wisdom from the angels when we ask for help.

What if I can already hear my angel? Why bother if they speak to me internally?

If you are at that level of communication, we applaud you! However, we find that this is a method that we use all the time along with channelings and other ways that we receive angelic messages.

Hearing the angels is the goal, of course. Memories can fail us, though. We can forget important elements of a message. Our wishes and preferences can find their way into remembered angelic dialogue. Over time, the memory may fade entirely.

Angel journaling offers clear instruction. It is written, so we can refer to it whenever you need to. It is a way to get information outside ourselves to gain a new perspective and clarity. It is easier to "hear" the voice of the writing to discern what it isn't our own. And it is also helpful in that it can clarify things for others as well, allowing you to offer messages of comfort that they can return to again and again.

Ready to start?

Directions for angel writing.
1. Quiet yourself.

2. Center.

3. Pray in your tradition, asking that you be surrounded by Love and that only Love enter in and that only Love is served. Call your guardian Angel to enlighten, guard, and guide you.

4. Write, perhaps a question or a greeting, to your angel.

5. Begin writing the answer. Do not edit, censor, think, reread, or try to anticipate what comes next. Just write.

It's a little like taking dictation, some say. Some hear what to write, some feel as though their hands just know what to write. It may come fluently, or perhaps it comes in fits and starts. Pictures may come.

Let what comes, come, without judging or questioning it. When it stops, thank your angel for its help. You'll know when it's over as it will feel "finished."

Read it, looking for the high and holy truths in what you have written. Trust that your angel has given you guidance, as you have asked in faith for it. Look over what you have written and you will find wisdom and guidance there.

Many people stare blankly at their question or greeting, unsure of what to expect. Do not expect your hand to move on its own; that is highly unlikely! What is more usual is for you to begin with some hesitation, perhaps writing, "Dear Angel..." and then feeling rather silly as you continue on, "Dear [Your name], thank you for your question..." As you do, however, the words come more surely and perhaps more quickly.

You may worry that you have made it up -- many people do.

Remember the writing exercise earlier? Go back to what you wrote in that exercise.

Can you see a difference? Did you feel a difference in the way the words flowed in the journaling exercise as opposed to writing a poem or directions?

If you are unsure, try another question for the angels, following the steps as outlined above once more. With practise you'll recognize the angel's expression as very different from your own way of writing.

How Do I know This Isn't Me?

Angel messages sound different from our own speech. They tend to repeat words and ideas for emphasis. "All is well. All is well," for example.

They may have different sentence structure or use words we may not normally use. Sometimes they sound a bit stilted or stuffy; others find the messages far more casual than they expected.

You will find after a while that angels bring values that may differ from our own. They tend to see the big picture, whereas we are concerned with the here and now and the issues at hand.

Sometimes you may ask about something bothering you, only to be told that we needn't be concerned. The angels may turn your attention to another matter, perhaps a related matter or underlying condition or even another issue entirely.

It isn't that angels ignore our concerns, but sometimes they tell us not to worry because the concern will be ok and then discuss something other topic. When that happens, pay attention to the turn in the message: angels do not waste our time, so whatever they discuss has significance for us and our lives.

The Angel journal takes the most work to master, but it is a very effective tool in accessing the timeless and endless loving guidance of our heavenly friends. The process is basically one of trust, and it is one that gets easier with practice. The trust gets easier, as well, when you begin to create a stockpile of messages.

Going back over them makes it easier for you to see the difference in various angels' styles of communicating. It becomes easier, too, to recognize that the writing is not your own style of communicating - or your own perspective.

Here is another exercise to try once you get a bead on the difference between your voice and that of your angel's:

Hearing Your Angel
You'll need a notebook and a pen for this exercise.
1. Quiet yourself.
Get into a comfortable position. Turn off the phone. Give yourself time to be with your angelic friend.

2. Center.
Take some deep breaths and allow yourself to settle and relax. As you feel peaceful, breath normally and enjoy the serenity throughout your being.

3. Pray.
You now create a holy space where only the highest and best comes to you. Surround yourself with white light and ask divinity to be with you. Ask your angel to come forward.

4. Ask your angel to guide you, asking a question if you wish. In this sacred space, you can unburden your heart. Your angel will never judge or condemn. They are with you to assist as they can.

5. Pay attention to what you receive or hear.

6. Having asked, treat what you have understood as holy.

7. Write about it in your notebook or journal so you don't forget. If you prefer, respond to the message received and begin a dialogue with your angel. When you have finished, record any insights or understandings that strike you as especially helpful as well as any you want to take to prayer or reflection.

All of these exercises will help you become more aware of the ways in which your angels communicate with you on a daily basis.

Deepening Your Relationship with Your Angel
Questions you may want to ask your angel in your journal:
    -What shall I call you?
(Note: angels don't have names as we do. They will give us a name of some kind for our convenience, however. That name will carry a vibration that is appropriate for the particular angel or have other significance.)
        -What is the best way for me to connect with you?
        -What do I need to know right now?
        -How can I best serve?
        -How can I bring more light and love into my life
    -How can I best express light and love?
        -How can I create more abundance in my life?
        -What are my lessons at this time?
        -What am I learning in the situation with _____?
        -How can I best express my creativity?
        -How can I achieve inner peace?
        -Where do I need to grow and develop?
    -What can I do to deepen my spiritual life?

Remember that your time with your angel is holy. Always begin with a prayer that surrounds you with God's light and love, then ask your question, record what comes, and say thanks. It really is that simple!

Inner Guidance

The most common way in which we hear our angel's voice is through inner guidance. And how do we know it is our dear angel's guidance?

There is a knowing, a recognition, an instant understanding. We call it the 'thud' effect; sometimes it is more of an 'in-your-face' recognition. A friend swears sometimes it's more like a whack on the side of the head, while Jean has a very familiar style of angelic interaction born of a lifetime of friendship with her guardian, and their 'conversations' often sound like dear friends' gentle bickering.

When you get an AHA! experience after asking a question or seeking clarity, then it is most likely angels bringing you reassurance and support. They work with us through our intuition, through those "gut feelings," through images, ideas, and inspirations that just won't go away. Angel Lady Deb's favorite way to receive messages is during through sleep, when she wakens with a solution to a nagging concern.

The world, siding with Common Sense and the "Seeing is Believing" principal, tends to downplay inspiration -- especially that which can be attributed angelically. We may have tended to ignore our inner guidance in the past, passing it off as our own ideas, wishful thinking, or daydreams.

Our inner critic may play havoc with the process for a while, until we get more comfortable with the information that comes to us. Remember our physical ego-self thinks it is protecting us by making us question what has come through -- and even whether it is possible at all to communicate with angels.

After working with these exercises and practising the journaling work, it will become more and more clear that you aren't just making all this up. And when you open the channels to receive your angel's guidance and inspiration, get ready. They have lots of ideas. They have LOTS of ways to keep you busy...so don't say you weren't warned!

Chapter 13 - Hearing Your Angels More Clearly

The most important thing the angels teach us is that if we ask, they answer; if we call, they come; if we request, they act. All we have to do is ask, call, or request in alignment with love - and they will respond. All we have to do then is recognize the angels in action. The recognition aspect can be tricky, frankly.

Like any relationship, if you want to get to know your angels, you have to spend time with them. It is VITAL to take time each day to connect, to meditate and to journal.

Some Common Blocks

Many people have difficulty connecting with their angels in the beginning. Here are some common reasons that may resonate with you.

Sometimes the reason lies in a simple misunderstanding. You may be missing their message because the angels do not look, work, or act as you may have thought. When the angels work, then, it's easy to discount actual angelic interaction as coincidence or, worse, nothing at all.

Our human emotions and reason can get in the way. Emotions like fear can keep our spiritual eyes closed as a protective measure. Impatience and a desire to control the interaction ("It MUST be this way...the angel MUST do this...") can also create frustration, since angels cannot be rushed or controlled.

Sometimes we want something too much. Like the child of fable who planted a seed and then dug it up each day to see if it had begun to grow, we can inadvertently fix our focus so tightly on the outcome that we fail to notice the steps that lead us to exactly what we want.

There is our human friend, ego. We want the right things, but we blend in a little vanity and muddy the waters. We don't just want a relationship, we want to get the most incredible messages right from the start. We don't just want to be aware of our angel, we want to have a vision that throws us into spontaneous ecstasy.

Part of our awareness is focused on the experience of working with our angel, but part is focused on ourselves as we do so. That certainly makes it hard to perceive accurately!

Many people do not believe themselves to be worthy of such a relationship. If angelic friendship seems to be something restricted to psychics or extremely holy people, many students will not believe themselves to be appropriate for such a holy friendship. Their expectation places them out of the angelic loop.

Those are some of the reasons. In our observation, the most common reasons people fail to perceive their angels in a satisfying way are these:
- they have been taught they are not good enough to see or speak with angels.
- they expect the angels to communicate with Cecil B. DeMille grandiosity.

Our experience is that, when people ask to become aware of angelic actions in their lives so that they may become more closely united to Love, angels never say no. And our experience is that angels rarely do the DeMille, movies excepted.

Block Breakers
So where does that leave you, if you have not yet had the experience you hoped to enjoy? Don't give up; it will happen for you. We are confident that it will. In fact, we are confident that it al-

ready HAS - you just haven't recognized it yet.

We suggest you keep working. Meditate daily - even if it's only for three minutes in the parking lot before you go into the office.

Give up your expectations. That doesn't mean stop expecting to meet your angel; it means stop expecting that you know what that will be like. Let go of how you think it will be, and work with what actually happens when you ask.

Make time for angel activities. Write in your journal, ask the angels to help others, write letters to your angel, listen. Make time for angel-writing, asking for messages, and note what you get and how you feel.

Beef up your inspirational reading. Reading about others' experiences of angels - can help you recognize your own more easily.

Reframe your desires. Bring them in line with angelic goals. That is, instead of asking that your neighbour be brought to his knees for playing music too loudly, ask that your loud neighbor be blessed with an appreciation of peace and quiet. You might ask that your neighbour be brought to a wonderful happy home even better than the one next door to yours – and that the new neighbors be perfect for the neighbourhood.

Angels bless; ask that you be blessed by their guidance so that you can better become a blessing on the earth.

There is no magic wand, no magic bullet that will suddenly open your eyes to an angelic world that surrounds you, unseen by others. To get to that place, you must pay your admission. What are you willing to give in order to have a relationship with your angels?
Maybe it's ten minutes of sleep, so you rise earlier each day to spend time in meditation and angel writing.

Maybe it's the idea that you're not much of a person after all, that you aren't the beloved child of the Most High but only a lowly human unworthy of an angel's attention, much less the Creator's undying and all-encompassing Love. (Please give that one up! It is so far from the truth of who you are and who each person is.)

You get the idea, we're sure.
Don't give up, and don't even work harder.

Instead, work the way the angels do, with perfect trust and love. Even when we turn our back on the way of Love, our angels never despair. They know that our path, even if it looks like the road to Hell, simply contains different lessons and will eventually find its way back to the one we meant to travel in the first place.

So keep at it, even when you aren't sure of the results. Be certain that it's simply a matter of time before the pieces fall into place and you feel your angel surrounding you with love and offering its messages of love and wisdom.

Chapter 14 - Enlisting the Angel's Help: A Powerful Activity

By this point, you've tried the activities, you've considered blocks and block breakers. Hopefully, you are starting to hear your angels a little more clearly and feeling comfortable that they are indeed with you and ready and willing to assist.

This is a fabulous exercise to get the angels working with you and helping you to manifest blessings and dreams.

You will need:
-Rubber Cement (or a gluestick)
-Scrap paper for gluing (to keep tabletop clean)
-Several magazines you enjoy, preferably glossy as opposed to pulp
-A pair of scissors suitable for cutting paper
-A trash can or bag
-Two manila folders or other heavy cardstock backings
  (Tip: dark coloured folders work better as they keep the words on the back of your images from showing through)
-Your angel journal or other paper(s)
-A pen
-Coloured markers, if you like

The Task: Creating an Angelic Active Intervention Diagram, or Angel Aid

An Angel Aid is a graphic representation those things with which you'd like angelic assistance in accomplishing. You've probably made dozens of New Year's Resolutions and turned more 'New

Leaves' than you'd care to count.

Often, those good intentions fall victim to procrastination, fear, doubt, and even forgetfulness. But if you had your angel working with you on those tasks, you'd have better chance of success, wouldn't you?

After all, your angel's chief goal is leading you along paths of goodness and Love, so whatever goals you set ... your angel will try valiantly to help you succeed with them - as long as those goals are in your highest and best interests.

That's right: if your goal serves Love, your angel will gladly assist, because your angel's first and deepest allegiance is to Love itself. Bearing that in mind, then, you will see that the task you complete this week is far more than simply making a collage or goal map.

Read all directions before beginning.

Physical Directions for Constructing your Angel Aid
One part of the task is simply to list the areas in your life that you want angelic help. For now, do not bother trying to see the future and whether each will work for good in your life. Just list the goals with which you want help.

Typical goals for this activity include (but are not limited to the following):

- Health goals (weight loss, smoking cessation, healthier lifestyle, faithfulness to exercise programs,etc.)

- Mundane goals (better job, increased salary, new home, a car that runs well, etc.)

- Mental goals (clarity around job or relationship issues, faster learning of concepts covered in school or training, ease in managing difficult people at work, etc.)

- Spiritual goals (new relationship, greater respect, clearer direction in life, increased spiritual understanding, flowering of spiritual gifts, understanding your life purpose and so on.)

You get the idea. Add new categories if you wish, or not. This is your list. When you have finished, select the five or seven most important goals. These become your active list - the priorities list for your angel.

Once you have made your list, open one folder so it lies flat. The inner sides of your folder will be your 'canvas.' Divide it into as many sections as you have goals. The sections do not have to be equal in size. A more important goal may get more space, others not. It's up to you.

You can label each segment with the goal you have chosen.

Now the fun begins. Leafing through your magazine, choose words, symbols and pictures that best represent the task you want help with and its successful outcome. For example, if you have chosen learning more easily, photos might include books, schools, and smiling people.

Clarity around career choices might include photos representing each of the choices facing you, someone to represent you, and someone to represent your family/friends cheering you on.

If you cannot find words you really want to include - or quotations - just use the pen or markers to neatly letter them on a page of writing paper or an extra page taken from your angel journal.

To make the task easier, you might get a bowl to represent each individual goal so that the words and pictures for your goals don't get mixed together. Just drop the clipped pictures or words into the appropriate bowl or container.

When you have enough, open the extra folder. On it, begin a sample layout which will later be transferred to the other folder and glued down.

Arrange and rearrange until you are satisfied with the placement of elements. Note: place largest pieces first, arranging smaller elements in the open spaces and over the larger pieces.

When you are satisfied, begin the transferring process. Simply take one area of the folder, gently slide out the largest items, and glue them down. Working from folder (or back of composition) to the top (or front), continue gluing the items down until you have completely recreated the goal-designs you made on your Angel Aid folder.

That is the mundane, physical part of the task. There's more.

Spiritual Directions for Constructing your Angel Aid
At the beginning, invite your angels to join you in the work. Ask them to help you think of goals and to select the ones with which to work.

Ask your angels to help you find words, phrases, letters and even pictures that depict the goals in mind - and their happy outcomes as well. Express your willingness to receive your angels' message as you work - to hear them, perhaps, or to recognize words and quotations that pierce your spirit with the loving truths they inspire.

While you are working, allow yourself to drift into that right-brained, contemplative state of mind that just *does* without over-thinking the process.

Allow yourself to become lost in the task at hand, finding the words and pictures, choosing quotations, creating the design, gluing the elements.

That's it. If you have any decoupage medium handy, you can use it for this project instead of the glue. Brush a coat over the whole thing when you finish - it will secure any loose edges and provide a protective surface to your composition.

When you have finished, bless it with a little prayer. Asking that it be a vehicle for your spiritual insight and understanding. Let the Aid sit for a day or so before you return to it, then take a long look.

Set it where you can look at it easily. See what thoughts and understandings come as you view it. Ask your angel to use it as a tool to offer you insight. Have your journal handy, and record any insights or inspirations or interesting ideas that it elicits from you - or that your angel shares with you.

You will be surprised by how such a mundane and ordinary task can be deeply meaningful - and a source of insights you do not expect! All you have to do is – do it, and be open to what comes.

$Part\ III$

Deeping Connections with Your Angels

This channeled Angel Message was given for the participants taking our course. We know that it will bless you too as you continue to work with your loving angels.

Most beloved children, welcome and welcome!
It is a delightful time, to mark the end of your period of study. It is the time to cast an eye over the many weeks prior and to reflect on all that you have gained.

You have all had the experience of earthly teachers and earthly school classrooms. You well understand the process of receiving conceptual information, of reading and discussing it until it becomes sensible to you, and then of reviewing it again and again until the concepts become part of your body of knowledge.

After all this comes the test. Now you must prove to the teacher's satisfaction that you understand the matter completely and have mastered the information so that it is always available to your recall. Following the test, you are assigned a grade that expresses how satisfactorily you have accomplished this task. It is a grueling and stressful task, learning in an earthly classroom!

Stressful though it is, such schooling is appropriate for human understandings of the world in which you live.

But you do not seek human understanding in this class.

Instead, you have sought angelic understanding: the Way of the Angels, after all. So it should be no surprise that this class has taken a form far different from that which you may have expected and even different from what your teachers expected as well.

Both of your teachers are true teachers in the earthly sense and so anticipated a course like those which they have studied throughout their years of education. This was quite right and proper and we thank them for their efforts in researching information from human sources and compiling it a format you could use.

That, however, was only the beginning.

For if you seek to walk in the way of the angels, then learning about angels from the human perspective is only the merest beginning of what there is to know. You must learn about people now, but from the angelic perspective!

To do so, you must learn about our motivations, our hopes and joys, our understanding of All that Is. You must not only learn these things but welcome them into your lives and your hearts.

And so, you dear children, what do you know of us and our ways?

You know, perhaps, that we serve Love. What does it mean, to serve Love? And what is Love, after all?

You understand love in a human way; how could you not? Love, then, becomes an affection born of pleasure. As another pleases you - in appearance, in actions or words, in personal qualities, in their appreciation of your own delightful self, perhaps even in the atmosphere one creates of danger or excitement - these pleasing moments generate feelings of pleasure.

You wish to enjoy more of these, and as you do, the feelings of pleasure become attached to the person themselves: you love them.

Sometimes the 'person' you love is not even a person but a cherished pet, perhaps, or activities or places which create similar feelings of pleasure, affirmation, and emotion. No matter. It is still an experience of love.

Those who teach the truths they have come to know through various religious disciplines have imparted those teachings to the world. In these teachings, love takes on a new character and that character varies depending on whose understandings you study.

Some focus on the sacrificial aspects of love. In such visions, love is akin to suffering for, if one loves, one gladly assumes the burdens of the loved one that the beloved's burden may be the lighter to carry. Certainly, it is true that when one loves on a human level, one wishes to ease the other's way.

Occasionally, though, in such teachings the value of the self is lost. The teaching becomes not so much to extend compassion to those one loves as to exhaust oneself for the benefit of others, expecting nothing in return. Sometimes the faithful are called even to refuse what is offered, choosing instead to suffer more greatly thereby.

Oh, dear! Such inconsistency!

For if all seek to give and not take, to whom, then, shall they give? And what burden of 'sin' would this impose on the hapless receiver, who enjoys gifts of service on earth only to burn in the hereafter for their selfishness!

Other systems focus on personal responsibility of each individual. Being given the gift of power to create your own lives, your first responsibility is to self. Therefore, others must tend their own gardens, for you are busy creating yours!

Some focus on legalistic approaches to love. Love means obeying the laws they accept as important and holy. Love, being the cornerstone of life, then codifies every aspect of life and woe to those who break the code!

Dear children. How hard you work to understand the mind of the Holy One! How willingly you give up the delights of the life you have been given, the better to draw near the heart of the Creator!

Peace, beloveds. Peace.

Love, the Creator, the Holy One, All That Is... is simple and incomprehensibly complex at once. For you, know that Love is supreme among all that has been created. Love has created from Loveself all that you see around you. There is only love.

You cannot separate yourself from it, although you can easily erect a screen through which Love may assume other appearances. Regardless of the glass through which Love is seen, Love is unchanging. Love does not operate under the laws you understand but is Loveself the law by which all things operate.

When you think of love, dear children, you think of the emotion you name 'love.' This is a beautiful emotion, certainly.

But Love is not an emotion but a living, vibrant entity, an energy that is found within everything that has been created. Here again, your language fails you, for 'energy' is something you regard as insentient and inanimate. Love is neither, but knows, feels, understands, and lives with an exquisite acuity you cannot hope to achieve. And so, you may well call Love, 'God' or 'Goddess.'

It is Love we serve. We serve Love by loving. We serve Love by being love, by loving All That Is, by loving you. We serve Love by acting in ways that support the aims of Love, which are to express the divine perfection of Love through all things by calling each to Loveself in sublime union.

We serve Love by allowing. We allow Love to be, we allow Love to flower, we allow Love to teach the unimaginable wisdom of Love's own ways to each of Love's children. We allow our very selves to strain toward that Love from which we spring, even as our tasks take us to the farthest reaches of the Universe you observe. As you seek to know our ways, here they are: In all, serve Love. To all, extend Love. Despite all, continue Love.

And now, dearest children, perhaps the question becomes how can you begin to walk in the way of angels?

The wisest of your spiritual teachers have offered models you may follow. Your teacher Jesus, who refused none his love and compassionate healing. Your teacher Schweitzer, who saw mirrored in the tiniest creature the unfathomable magnificence of Love. Your teacher Ghandi, whose fearless dedication to peace and justice have inspired generations of your people.

Think of Hildegarde, whose very heart sang with the music of Love echoing through the starry wasteland of the Universe. Remember Kwan Yin, the divine mother who would not enter nirvana with even a single child left behind. And Mary, the model of perfect trust in the perfect outworking of Love.

There are hundreds and millions of teachers from whom you will learn more and more of love. Even the rocks themselves can teach you much, should you listen for their wisdom.

As you work with us, as you call to us for insight and direction, we are there at your side. Always, we are eager to lead you into a deeper union with Love, your source and end. Let your words and thoughts be formed by the understanding you have gained that you may walk in peace, drawing by your gentle spirit those who have need of Love's tender compassion and finding at every hand the gifts of Love showered upon you!

Know that your angels are filled with joy by your earnest wish to be so led.

Chapter 15 - The Importance of Meditation

When people come to our workshops, they often have an unrealistic expectation that by the end of the day they will be on an intimate and easy basis with their angels. While angel workshops allow people the opportunity to learn how to communicate with the angels, that kind of easy intimacy takes time to develop.

As you have worked through this book, we have offered tools to develop a relationship with your angels and given some background to help you understand who they are and their purpose in our lives. As we work with angels it brings us to a new understanding of our world - both physical and spiritual. This spiritual component is critical in developing a full connection with the angels around us.

Angels are beyond religion. They are beyond time and space. They are created to protect us, guide us, assist us, and walk with us as we journey through life. The only reason that they are with us is because our Creator has sent them to us and their fidelity to Creator and their obedience to that Loving Will means that they are steadfast in their care for us. Creator loves us so much that we've been given the gift of these heavenly assistants, and the angels love Creator so much that they say yes to the task of hanging out with each of us 24/7 throughout our life.

So, when we connect with our angels, we are also connecting to Divinity. We cannot speak with angels without hearing the Creator mirrored back. That is why the message of an angel is only loving, caring, guiding, uplifting. Creator speaks through them to us.

An angel will never take any credit or praise because everything they do is to glorify Divine Love.

As we come to know our angels more fully and appreciate the blessings they bring into our lives, we will find ourselves wanting to spend more time connecting with them. Setting aside a time to meditate each day is an excellent way to receive those loving vibes.

Some people react negatively to the word "meditation." For some it has been a difficult exercise and a frustrating waste of time. Nothing seems to happen. Thoughts cannot be shut down. Minutes seem like hours. We've been there, too.

If you have had limited experience with meditation, there are some fears and concerns that come to our attention, particularly among communities which regard influences from other cultures as dangerous. It has not been our experience that members of these communities are drawn to the angels generally or our work in particular.

But if you have been raised in a traditional background, you may have been given mixed messages about the appropriateness of meditation. Certainly silent prayer and reflection on words from a holy book or from a holy person has been a practice of the Christian community, but there has been a hesitance to embrace the meditation techniques of other cultures.

While meditation has long been part of the Christian tradition (for example, the rosary or the Jesus Prayer), it became highly popular many years ago when singers like the Beatles began practicing a particular type of meditation, Transcendental Meditation, developed by Marishi Mahesh Yogi.

The Angel Ladies do not practice Transcendental Meditation and have a very limited understanding of it. We do not teach TM or promote it, just as we do not promote any religious traditions with their layers of richness and history. We respect all and promote none.

We do, however, make use of visualization and relaxation as we work with our angels. Our purpose is to allow the angels to communicate to us through insight and imagery.

Our meditations are not deep trance-like meditation such as those you see on television, where a practitioner in trance might be oblivious as s/he is poked with pins. Instead, we seek a relaxation that does not block out the world around us; if the fire alarm goes off or the cat knocks over a glass of water, we want to hear it and respond appropriately.

Dangers of Meditation

Can opening oneself to spirits be dangerous? Dangerous is a strong word, but we agree that it is not a beneficial or healthy practice to open oneself to any and all spirits. Think of a Ouija board - users simply place their hands on the planchette and ask a spirit to speak. Because of this broadcast invitation, most people in the psychic community steer clear of Ouija.

When meditation is not grounded in the spiritual practise of the user, it is like using a Ouija board or broadcasting an invitation to anyone inclined to 'drop in.' That is never wise, and we believe that such an activity could produce undesirable or even harmful results.

Whenever one elects to practice meditation - even the simple form advocated by our angels of 'Sitting in the Silence' - care is warranted, always.

Protection

How do we protect ourselves from evil spirits, fallen angels, wayward entities, earth-bound souls, etc?

For us, the simplest way is to align our will with that of the Creator and to invoke the protection of our Guardian Angels. This is an ancient belief of Christians. Theodoret of Cyr (393-466) in his Interpretation of Daniel wrote, "We are taught that each one of us is entrusted to the care of an individual angel to guard and protect us, and to deliver us from the snares of evil demons." Christian belief in a Guardian Angel finds support in

Jesus's words, "I say to you that their angels in heaven always look upon the face of my heavenly Father." (Mt 18)

Aligning our will with that of the Creator can be as simple as a prayer we have learned from childhood or as elaborate as an entire ritual of consecration. We often say, "May all done in Love, for Love, and through Love, that Divine Love may be served." Love is one of our names for Divinity, the Creator, God, the Holy One, etc.

Invoking the protection of our Guardian Angels is even easier. Jean simply issues a mental call to her guardian. You may feel more comfortable being more explicit, "My Angel, I ask you to surround me with your protective love, casting far from me anything which is not of Love/God/etc., and protecting me from all dark spirits and energies."

As part of Jean's Catholic upbringing, she learned the prayer to St. Michael the Archangel: "St. Michael, the Archangel, defend us in battle. Be our protection against the wickedness and snares of the devil; May God rebuke him, we humbly pray, and thou, O Prince of heavenly host, by the power of God, thrust into hell Satan and all evil spirits who wander through the world for the ruin of souls. Amen." It is a powerful and long-respected prayer of protection.

And every Catholic child learned the Guardian Angel prayer: "Angel of God, my guardian dear, to whom God's love entrusts me here, ever this day be at my side to light, to guard, to rule and guide. Amen."

Protective elements from other traditions include smudging with sage, an ancient form of clearing and protecting. Other old techniques of protection and clearing include sprinkling salt or holy water, lighting candles, clapping sharply three times, ringing bells or chimes, or surrounding oneself in white light.

In our daily life, we often light candles. We connect to Love, that is, we pray throughout the day. We smudge before and after events and when we feel the nudge. When Deborah presides at house blessings, she calls the guardians of the house and other angels to create a shield through which only Love, only light, only goodness may enter in.

Most religious and spiritual traditions include rituals or ceremonies of blessing and protection, and we encourage people to use them often. Which to use? We recommend students use the practices that feel holiest and most powerfully protective to them.

Your Time of Meditation
All that said, taking time for daily meditation is time well-spent. You can expect not only a greater peace and spiritual understanding over time, but also decreases in stress and blood pressure. And, like the old proverb, your day is likely to go better when it is 'hemmed' by such reflection.

By opening yourselves to Divine Spirit in this way, you are energized by divine Love and blessed. You receive comfort and reassurance, become uplifted and supported by Love. You cannot regularly spend time in this blessed state without experiencing changes in attitude; your outlook, response, and perspective reflect your growing enlightenment by Love.

When should you do your meditations?
Short answer: whenever you like. Your angel is always with you, whether you know it or not, so you'll never receive a busy signal.

Choose a time when you are most likely to be faithful to the practice. If your mornings are hectic, perhaps after dinner is a better time. If evenings are taken up by homework with the children, it might be that a few minutes at the office work best. Lunchtime spent outdoors offers an opportunity, but so does a quiet time in your car in the parking tower before heading home.

If you already have a prayer or reflection time as part of your daily routine, including a few extra minutes to request angelic guidance is a wonderful addition to that special part of your day. As your angel's 'voice' or manner becomes more familiar to you, you will be able to request your angel's guidance throughout every day. Even better, you'll be able to recognize your angel as it offers you guidance unbidden.

How long should you spend in the meditations?
As long as you like. Your angel will not judge you for taking too long or not long enough. On the other side, there is no time - it is a fact of human life but not spiritual life - so whatever time you take will be perfectly adequate.

Same Time, Same Place?
Your angel doesn't care if you use the same time of day and the same place for your meditations. Your angel is always at hand, so it's never inconvenient for your angel.

On the other hand, having a routine of meditation is very helpful for us humans. Being creatures of habit, knowing that every day as the sun sets our task is to walk over to the park or backyard bench for angel time is very helpful to us. Routines make it easier for us not to give up good habits as we try to incorporate them into our lives.

Helpful Preparations
Choose a time when you will be undisturbed.
If you find that candles and soft music help you to relax and better connect to things spiritual, by all means, light a candle and play suitable music.

You may wish to decorate for the occasion, setting a corner of your room as a meditation area. You might place symbols or images to remind you of divine Love; you may enjoy fresh flowers. A comfortable chair is always a good idea.

Having notebooks and pens on hand is also a good idea. You can use them to jot down those ideas that won't leave your mind, making it easier to become mentally silent. As you meditate or directly afterward, you may want to note insights you received.

Beginning

Ground and center. You can begin simply by taking a few deep breaths, allowing your mind to become quiet and peaceful. Turn your attention to Love and invite your angel to help your connection to the Divine.

You may say any prayer that is meaningful to you. Or, if you prefer, you may speak in the quiet of your heart. Offer your concerns and ask Love's protection and guidance.

Read something to inspire you - prayers, holy passages, etc. Consider any insights that come as you read it. Perhaps something will strike your spiritual ear differently. If so, note it. You may receive an image; in that case, sketch it out. You might feel impressed to dance or sing; do so. Then again, you may just want to read it and then breathe deeply, sitting in the silence of Love. There is no wrong way to begin.

Calling on Your Angel

Turn your attention to your angel after a short meditation. Ask for guidance or messages; record what comes. Remember that what comes may be words, memories, images, feelings, sensations, or even tastes or smells.

Remember that anything that comes to you from your angel will NEVER reflect condemnation or judgement. If you feel these coming through, quiet your mind once more. These feelings may come from self, particularly the self that likes things orderly and just-so, or they may be old tapes playing messages you have received and internalized from others. Either way, they are not a reflection of where you stand in the eyes of your angel or God.

Bring forward any concerns you may have, ask any questions you like. ALWAYS record what you ask and what you receive, even if it seems to make no sense. Often, after you have time to sit with it, the pieces fall into place.

Intercede for others at this time. Send angels to help victims of violence or natural disaster, to help the planet or its creatures. Whatever causes or needs are important to you, your angel can help. You can call a million million angels to assist in whatever areas you like. As long as you couch your request in terms of light and love, as opposed to control and judgement, your angels will always hasten to help at your request.

Ending Your Session

When you are finished, merely thank your angel for its care. Thank Love for the blessings that fill your life. And that's it!

So, in a nutshell:
1. Set your intention: to grow in Love and understanding, to align with Love/God/Good, to receive the blessings of the angels Love has given you as a protector and guide back to Love.

2. Complete protection: state mentally or verbally your intention that you act in Love, that you are divinely protected, that the guardian angel given you by Love acts as the Creator has decreed to keep you safe from all darkness and danger.

3. Engage in your meditative practice, whether it is a taped visualization, a silent meditation, repetition of a mantra, etc.

4. Thank Love/God/etc for the time of union and blessing and offer blessing to the world.

Chapter 16 - A Week with the Angels

Here for your use is A Week with the Angels, a weeks' worth of reflections that many have found helpful.

Day One

You may simply wish to open in prayer, skip the reflection and speak to your angel. That's perfectly okay, but for those who like more structure to their prayer time, we offer this day-by-day outline as a suggestion. Before long, you will adapt your daily angel time in the way that is most helpful to you.

Prepare your Sacred Space

Play soft music, light a candle, display icons and meaningful symbols, have a book and pen at hand. Choose a comfortable place to sit or recline.

Opening Prayer

Take some deep breaths. Relax. Allow your heart and mind to welcome the peaceful presence of Loving Creator. Invite the Creator and your Guardian Angel to be with you throughout this time of prayer and reflection. Your prayer can be formal or a simple invitation for God's love to be made known in your life on this day. The important thing is to unite with Love as we proceed.

Time of Meditation

Read the following, or, if you prefer, read another passage, prayer, poem that is conducive to self-reflection.

Meditation: What If

When something is worrying us, it's hard to put it aside. Those "what-ifs" just won't let us alone, it seems. Even worse, the fears they generate often paralyze us, preventing us from taking action to handle the original problem.

Here's a helpful technique often credited to Dale Carnegie. Take five minutes to consider your own worst-case scenario, the "what-if" that makes your stomach clench. Now, make a plan. What will you do if worse comes to worst? If the boss really does hate you, then what? If your marriage really does end, if you really can't pay your bills this month--what next? There are steps you can if the worst happens. Make a plan, just in case.

Once you do so, the what-ifs lose their power. It's amazing how free you'll become to focus on solutions so that your worst-case plan is never needed after all. Having a plan takes away the fear that "what-ifs" create. "If this happens, I'll just do that....and if that happens, I can always do this. I may not want to, but I can if I have to." Just knowing that there's something else you can do has a tremendously calming effect. Try it and see!

Going Deeper: Response to the Meditation
What insights come as you reflect on this short meditation? How does this apply to your life? What memories or situations come to mind? Work with the insights and express them in the manner that is most effective for you. (Record them, draw, move, continue to quietly reflect)

Call on Your Angel
Ask for further insights from your Angel that might be of benefit for you to know and understand.

Record anything that you receive. Spend time with your angel in prayer, listening for direction, asking for guidance and assistance, sending angels to help those in need....

Traditional Prayer to the Guardian Angel
Angel of God, my guardian dear
To whom God's love commits me here,
Ever this day be at my side
To light and guard, to rule and guide. Amen

Thank your angel and our loving God for all the blessings you have received. Offer a concluding prayer such as the Lord's Prayer or one that expresses your gratitude and willingness to serve.

Final Prayer

Heavenly One, it is true that you never close a door without opening a window. There is always a way to handle any challenge we face. Send angels to open my eyes to the options I have so that I may face each day unafraid and secure in the knowledge that all will be well!

Affirmation

A thought to keep with you as a reminder that all is well as you move through your busy day:

With God's help, I know I will find my way through any difficulty I face.

Day Two

Prepare your Sacred Space

Opening Prayer

Loving God, I welcome you now into my heart. Holy Angel surround me in the embrace of your love that I might be open to guidance and assistance in this time of prayer. Thank you for your many blessings. Amen

Meditation: Expect a Miracle

What's that, you say? A miracle? Maybe we need to redefine miracles, for no one expects the seas to part that you may pass through to a happier life. But miracles--the unexpected and sometimes inexplicable appearance of just what is needed at the time--do happen, even in our sophisticated and jaded world.

A friend remembers a time when she was genuinely out of money, with only a few dollars to last until the end of the month. She prayed, then took her remaining dollars to purchase what food she could. After making her careful purchases, she returned to her car, there to find a wad of bills on the ground beside it!

She counted: ninety dollars, a great sum to her at that time. She waited and waited, but no one came by retracing their steps as they searched for lost money. She notified the grocer, but no one ever inquired. The money saw her through a very difficult month.

Another friend remembers an unexpected job opportunity out of the blue. A third recalls a chance conversation that led to just the information she needed to solve a troublesome problem.

Such "garden-variety" miracles occur every day. You may have experienced one or more of them yourself, in fact! When things get tense, recall that God's love is unlimited and that God's help always finds its way to us!

Going Deeper: Response to the Meditation

Do you believe in miracles? Have you experienced one? In what area of your life do you need help and hope? What would constitute a miracle for you?

Call on Your Angel
Activity: Hearing your angel

Quiet yourself and center. Pray, then ask to hear clearly your angel's guidance. Ask your question, then pay attention to what you hear, trusting that it is the answer to your prayerful request. Then write it down so you won't forget what you received. Trust the wisdom you find in your answer.

Spend time offering intercessory prayers, if desired. Conclude with the Lord's Prayer or the following:

Heavenly friend, my own guide and guardian, be always and ever at my side. Help me to hear your voice, recognize your inspirations, and follow your direction as you lead me daily to live a life of love and trust in the Holy One. Amen.

Final Prayer

Heavenly One, no problem is too great or too small for your love to solve. Let your angels open my eyes to the miracles taking place around me every moment.

Affirmation for the Day

God provides what I need when I need it. I welcome miracles into my life!

Day Three

Preparing your Sacred Space

Opening Prayer
Gracious God, I give you thanks for this gift of time to share with you. I give you thanks for the gift of my life and the journey that I travel with my beloved angel companion. Speak to my heart, and show me the ways in which I am called into wholeness this day. Amen

Meditation
Our deepest fear is not that we are inadequate. Our deepest fear is that we are powerful beyond measure. It is our light, not our darkness, that most frightens us. We ask ourselves, who am I to be brilliant, gorgeous, talented and fabulous? Actually, who are you not to be? You are a child of God.

Your playing small doesn't serve the world. There is nothing enlightened about shrinking so that other people will not feel insecure around you. We were born to make manifest the glory of God that is within us. It is not just some of us; it is in everyone.

And as we let our own light shine, we unconsciously give people permission to do the same. As we are liberated from our own fear, our presence automatically liberates others.
–Marianne Williamson, A Return to Love

Response to the Meditation
Do you feel that this is true for you? Do you let your light shine? Do you encourage others to shine their own light? What is this passage saying to you today? What action can you take to be a light in the world? What does "living in the light" mean to you?

Call on Your Angel

What insights come from your angel? How will your angel assist your light to shine more brightly? Ask your angel and record what you receive.

Spend time with your angel and share your concerns. Ask for guidance and assistance. Record any words or thoughts that come to you.

Spend time in intercessory prayer, if desired. Send angels to those who are in need of healing and help.

Conclude with this beautiful version of the Lord's Prayer from the New Zealand Book of Common Prayer, or one of your own preference.

Eternal Spirit, Earth-maker, Pain-bearer, Life-giver,
Source of all that is and that shall be,
Father and Mother of us all,
Loving God, in whom is heaven:
The hallowing of your name echo throughout the universe
The way of your justice be followed by the peoples of the world!
Your heavenly will be done by all created beings!
Your commonwealth of peace and freedom sustain our hope and come on earth.
With the bread we need for today, feed us.
In the hurts we absorb from one another, forgive us.
In times of temptation and test, strengthen us.
From trials too great to endure, spare us.
From the grip of all that is evil, free us.
For you reign in the glory of the power that is love,
now and forever.

Final Prayer

Holy One, I give you thanks for the gift of this world, the gift of my life, the gift of the blessings and challenges that serve to help me on my path. I call on your holy angels to open my heart to ways in which I can offer my gifts and talents to the good of all. This day I offer the treasure that I am to greater service, blessed to be a blessing, offered with joy and celebration.

Affirmation

I am a marvelous creation, fashioned by a generous and abundant Creator.

I celebrate the gifts that I have and the gifts that I have been given!

Day Four

Preparing your Sacred Space

Opening Prayer

Holy One, source of all light and goodness, pour your loving spirit upon me in this sacred time of prayer. May I be aware of your gentle inspiration and guidance given through my Guardian Angel. I give you thanks and praise. Amen.

Meditation

Luke 12: 22- 34 (NRSV)

Jesus said to his disciples, "Therefore I tell you, do not worry about your life, what you will eat, or about your body, what you will wear. For life is more than food, and the body more than clothing.

Consider the ravens: they neither sow nor reap, they have neither storehouse nor barn, and yet God feeds them. Of how much more value are you than the birds! And can any of you by worrying add a single hour to your span of life? If then you are not able to do so small a thing as that, why do you worry about the rest?

Consider the lilies, how they grow: they neither toil nor spin; yet I tell you, even Solomon in all his glory was not clothed like one of these. But if God so clothes the grass of the field, which is alive today and tomorrow is thrown into the oven, how much more will he clothe you -- you of little faith!

And do not keep striving for what you are to eat and what you are to drink, and do not keep worrying. For it is the nations of the world that strive after all these things, and your Father knows that you need them. Instead, strive for his kingdom, and these things will be given to you as well.

"Do not be afraid, little flock, for it is your Father's good pleasure to give you the kingdom. Sell your possessions, and give alms. Make purses for yourselves that do not wear out, an unfailing treasure in heaven, where no thief comes near and no moth destroys.

For where your treasure is, there your heart will be also.

Response to the Meditation
As you reflect on this passage and listen to the voice of Jesus, what emotions bubble up inside? What are worries on your heart? What are the ways in which you have known God to resolve and help you in the past? Take some time to list the many ways this passage speaks to you today. What action can you take to make your life healthier and happiest?

Call on Your Angel
Throughout your life you have experienced challenging times that caused worry and hardship. Many times, situations resolved themselves as though they were choreographed. It is certain that your angels had a hand in their happy resolution. Sometimes as we reflect over events in the past, new information comes to us. Write these down and look at their outcomes with fresh understanding.

You may ask your angel for clarity and assistance with any need you may have. Direct your angel and tell it how you would like things to proceed -- with harm to none, of course -- then leave it with your angel to assist with the detail work.

Take time for intercessory prayer, if desired. Call on angels to assist people in their needs; send angels to help in any situation. Nothing is too little or too large for them to handle.

Thank your angel and conclude with the Lord's Prayer or a prayer of thanksgiving and gratitude from your heart.

Final Prayer

Dear God, You understand how small we are and how large our problems loom in our thoughts. For us, they are more than we can handle, but for You they are specks of dust. Show me how to release each burden into your loving care. Holy Angel, be a quiet voice in my heart, reminding me that I have a Creator who willingly takes my burdens from me if only I allow it.

Affirmation

Today I choose to let go and let God handle the problems that face me.

I choose to trust the goodness of God!

Day Five

Prepare your Sacred Space

Opening Prayer
As I come into your presence, I pray for wisdom and clarity. May God grant me the serenity to accept the things I cannot change, courage to change the things I can, and the wisdom to know the difference. May your holy Angel enlighten my mind in this time of prayer. Amen

Meditation:
In the attitude of silence, the soul finds the path in a clearer light, and what is elusive and deceptive resolves itself into crystal clearness. Our life is a long and arduous quest after Truth. There is more to life than increasing its speed. --Mahatma Ghandi

Response to the Meditation
What in your life needs clarifying? Some will laugh and reply, "What doesn't!" Think on your journey to this point in time.
What have you learned to be the truth of who you are?
What are the qualities about yourself that your love most?
What are the things that you would like to change?
What is the clear light that draws you into truth?
What feeds and nurtures you?
Re-read Ghandi's quote and drink in the words. What does it say to you today in the place where you find yourself?

Call on Your Angel
Ask your angel to offer any further insights into your reflection. You may ask your angel to help you as you struggle with some of these thoughts. Write down any images, words, or phrases that might come to your mind. Reflect on what the message is for you.

Offer prayers on behalf of those who need joy in their lives, for whom light and truth are elusive. Send angels to help them find the path that will lead them to Love and wholeness.

Conclude with a prayer of thanksgiving to God and your faithful heavenly friend.

Final Prayer

Loving God, today I offer my life to your great purpose and all-knowing wisdom. Even when all around me seems painful and broken, I will look for your love to help me through. Send your angels to guard and guide me. Help me to go with the flow and trust that everything will work out to the good.

Affirmation

I let go and let God. I trust in the higher plan.

Day Six

Prepare your Sacred Space

Opening Prayer

Eternal God, I open my being to your loving presence. I ask that your spirit would empower and inspire me in this time of prayer. I call on my heavenly counsellor to help me as I enter into prayer. In all things may I be aware of your will and your purpose. Amen

Meditation

Psalm 91 (NRSV)

You who live in the shelter of the Most High, who abide in the shadow of the Almighty, will say to the LORD, "My refuge and my fortress; my God, in whom I trust." For he will deliver you from the snare of the fowler and from the deadly pestilence; he will cover you with his pinions, and under his wings you will find refuge; his faithfulness is a shield and buckler.

You will not fear the terror of the night, or the arrow that flies by day, or the pestilence that stalks in darkness, or the destruction that wastes at noonday. A thousand may fall at your side, ten thousand at your right hand, but it will not come near you.

You will only look with your eyes and see the punishment of the wicked. Because you have made the LORD your refuge, the Most High your dwelling place, no evil shall befall you, no scourge come near your tent.

For he will command his angels concerning you to guard you in all your ways. On their hands they will bear you up, so that you will not dash your foot against a stone. You will tread on the lion and the adder, the young lion and the serpent you will trample under foot.

Those who love me, I will deliver; I will protect those who know my name. When they call to me, I will answer them; I will be with them in trouble, I will rescue them and honor them. With long life I will satisfy them, and show them my salvation.

Response to the Meditation
How does this beautiful psalm speak to you? What images came to you? What thoughts fed your heart? Do you trust that God has given your Guardian Angel and all manner of helpers to assist you through the course of your life? In what ways do you need protection and sanctuary this day?

Call on Your Angel
Ask you angel for further insights with regard to the reflection. Record what comes to you. Many times your angel has been there to assist and protect you in ways that you've noticed, and in many others that have seemed like coincidences.... List coincidences you have experienced. Could your angel have engineered them? Trust your intuition. If you feel doubt, it was probably not your angel. Angel nudges are usually accompanied by moments of realization that something very special has occurred.

If you wish, send angels to everyone you know. Send angels to those with whom you are experiencing conflict and ask them to negotiate a happy resolution. Then watch what happens!

Final Prayer
Loving Creator, You know the many dangers that threaten your people. You know the fear that sometimes fills my heart and weighs down my spirit. Help me to grow in trust that I am ever safe in your loving care. Dear Angel, when I am bowed down with worry, speak words of comfort to me, reassuring me that my Loving Creator is quick to protect me from all harm.

Affirmation
Today I choose to let go and let God handle the problems that face

me.
I choose to trust the goodness of God.

Day Seven

Prepare your Sacred Space

Opening Prayer

God of the cosmos, you who have at once created the vast universe and the mustard seed, be with me. Loving One, who knows me intimately and accepts me completely, I give thanks for your abundant blessings. May this time of prayer with you and my beloved angel be fruitful and helpful, that I might gain insight and serve you in love. Amen.

Meditation

Receiving Forgiveness

Once there were two brothers who lived in a small town. They owned a business together that was very prosperous. One day the older brother said something that wounded the younger deeply. They had a bitter argument and from that day onwards never spoke directly to each other again.

Twenty years passed and the elder brother took sick. With time running out, the family finally convinced the younger brother to visit. When he came to his brother's bedside, they burst into tears. As they looked at each other, they could not remember what had caused such bitterness and schism. In that moment, they embraced and apologized. When the brother died later that day, the remaining sibling grieved not only for the loss of a loved one, but for all those wasted years.

This story is not all that uncommon. Stubbornness, pride, hurt feelings can act like a wedge. Experiences can deeply wound and shake us. Often there is no recognition of the wrong or any way to resolve the feelings that can build and fester inside.

If we cannot get satisfaction or an apology that can restore balance, then for the sake of our own health and well-being, we must get to a place where the circumstance no longer has power over us. We might need loving help along the way, but wholeness can be ours if we but learn to let go and let God.

Response to the Meditation

How does this story speak to you? Who has hurt you most? Whom have you hurt most? Can you think of a trusted friend or counsellor that can help you resolve the situation and restore a sense of completion and peace, or is the situation one in which it is best to forgive and let go? What does this story say to you today? What direction do you need to work for reconciliation in your life?

Call on Your Angel

Take a few deep breaths and close your eyes. Ask your angel to speak to your heart. Listen very carefully to any words that come to you. Take note of special words of encouragement, comfort, and guidance. Perhaps an idea or an image will pop into your mind. Be aware of any leadings and write them down.

Think of the damage that holding onto such negative feelings can cause over time. Think about the way in which it can colour perception and attitude. Even opportunities to move forward into joyful situations can be stalled because of our state of mind.

Ask your angel to help you clear the hurt and negative feelings, knowing that this is a process that happens over time. Make a commitment this day to embrace love and a positive outlook, then watch your world change as a result!

Call to mind those people who have hurt you and those whom you have hurt or offended in any way. Send angels with the prayer that all would be reconciled according to God's plan and purpose and that valuable lessons would be understood for the good of all concerned. Give it to God and the powerful team of angels that work for healing and reconciliation.

Offer a prayer for all people in need or distress. Send angels to tend to them and bring you insights regarding your own path to healing. Give thanks and praise for all that God is doing in your life to free you from the negatives!

Final Prayer

Holy One, I ask your angels to help me let go of the anger and the hurt that I still carry about situations in my life. Help me to let go and let you restore healing, peace and balance.

Affirmation

I release and I relax with the help of my angels!

Chapter 17 - A Meditation to Meet Your Angel

Use the script which follows to record this meditation to help you become aware of your angel's action in your life to the present time.

Simply read the script slowly and gently, then play it ideally before retiring or when you have time to devote to this. Each ellipsis (...) indicates a pause. When you come to the dots, pause for a count of 3-5 before continuing to read. **Please note that this script is protected by copyright. You may not share or sell it in any form without written permission from The Angel Ladies.**

Becoming Aware of Your Angel (*Note: use your name every now and then; this is highly effective*)

_____, take this time to relax, let your body settle into a comfortable position as you prepare to relax very deeply.
Take a deep breath in and hold for a few beats, then release ... again ...
hold and release ... again, hold and release, relaxing deeply.
With every breath out ... feel your body relax a little more ... every breath in ... brings peace and calm ...every breath out releases more and more tension, anxiety, concern ... just breath comfortably and continue to relax, _____.

Imagine a small puffy cloud over your head ... Let it swirl around you and caress you ... moving slowly down, acting like a sponge to remove all the tension from your body ... Feel it softly moving

over your head, relaxing the muscles ... moving down and taking all the tension out of your jaws ... your face ... your eyes
leaving you more and more relaxed ... feeling so warm and comfortable ... feel it drift around your throat ... absorbing all the tightness and stiffness there ... let your throat soften and let go of the tension, relax ...

Now feel the puffy cloud at your shoulders ... absorbing the tension carried there ... feel your shoulders respond now ... Perhaps they relax and drop ... feeling warmth flow into them, untying the knots ... smoothing and relaxing as you breath in peace and breath out tension ... letting the gentle cloud help clear it away

Now your back and your arms are relaxing ... feel the muscles soften and release all the tightness.... let it go ... and let warmth and peace flow in its place...

And now the little cloud is at your chest and moving down to your abdomen ... let it absorb all the tension ... all the tightness ... all the worries and concern you store there ... as you breathe ... feel warmth and soothing feelings flow there ... let yourself relax.

Now the cloud is at your lower back and hips ... just let those powerful muscles relax ... let the sofa or bed hold you up .... feel supported by it ... cradled ... safe and protected and warm.
Feel the cloud absorb all your tensions ... and feel your muscles relaxing in response.

Now the cloud is moving over your legs ... and your muscles respond and soften ... as the tension drains away ... and the cloud moves over your knees.....down your calves to your ankles ... feel warmth flow through you ... and let the cloud take away the tightness ... relax and breathe.

And now the cloud is at your feet ... resting there gently... hovering and absorbing all the tension ... in all those small muscles ... in your toes ... arch ... heel. Now imagine that all the tension that remains ... is flowing out through your toes ... and is being taken away by this cloud. ... See it getting smaller and smaller .... imagine it fading ... and watch all your tension ... and worries ... and concern ... fade away. ... Your whole body is warm and relaxed ... you are alert, and comfortable ... fully supported by the sofa or bed holding you. ____, you are safe ... secure ... protected ...

In this most holy space, relaxing relax in such comfort and peace, turn your attention to the holy guardian angel given to you by our loving Creator.

Your angel is pure love, as is God. Your angel wishes for you only the love and the peace of our creator God, and it is your angel's great delight to lead you along
the path marked out for you by your loving God before the beginning of time.
____, you are now aware of your angel's presence beside you.

Always your angel has been at your side. Many times throughout your life, your has angel assisted you in ways you could not imagine.

As you drift in quiet peace, ask your angel now to recall to your mind ... in a very peaceful and comforting manner ... a time when you received such divine assistance ....
(When recording, pause 5 – 10 minutes here)

Be open to whatever memories will come...........................
(When recording, pause 5 – 10 minutes here)

Ask your angel to help you to recognize ... peacefully and calmly ... the many times you have been helped by loving angelic intervention................

(When recording, pause 5 – 15 minutes here)

Thank your angelic friend ... ... for all the support and gentle guidance ... ... that has been given to you.

Your angel is ever at your side ... eager to guide and assist you ... and longing to be of ever-greater help to your soul. ... Whenever you have a need, ... your angel is at hand ... and you need only turn to this loving friend ... to again receive help, ... comfort, ... consolation, ... and guidance.

In a moment, ... this beautiful time will come to an end ... with a count to 5. When the count ends, _____ you may either return to the present ... or, if appropriate, go to sleep.

One– when you awaken ... now or after an appropriate sleep period ... you bring with you the feelings ... of comfort and peace that you have enjoyed during this meditation. ......

Two- you awaken ... feeling fine and healthy ... energized and happy.

Three - you have an awareness of your angel's help ... throughout your life and ... when other memories of your angel's help arise ... you receive them peacefully and comfortably.

Four - on the next count ... you will either come to the present ... fully refreshed and energized ... feeling wonderful and happy... or you will drift into a wonderfully restful and healing sleep ... Sfrom which you will awaken feeling refreshed and revitalized.

Five.

Chapter 18 - That's a Wrap

This book serves as a guide for our Way of the Angels certification course. For over 20 years, we have been assisting people to get to know the angels present in their lives and to connect with that Spiritual realm that is greater than we can ever know.

Angels bring us a sense of hope, of possibilities, of Creator at work in our lives. We are reminded of our worth and of the unlimited love available to us. Angels love us so much because Creator, who cherishes each and every one of us, has given them to us.

They are with us because they are dedicated to Divine Love and are obedient to that request. Your angels are with you to guide, inspire, and help you in the journey.

As you become more aware of your angels and more secure in your relationship with them, you'll find yourself including them as part of your life more and more. You'll find that you are more aware of blessings. And, as a natural extension of that, a willingness to reach out and bless others and the world.

How do you do that? Simply by calling on the angels to help. Say you are watching a horrible scene unfolding in the news - send angels to help everyone in need and bring a swift comfortable resolution to the situation.

Or perhaps you hear about someone who is ill, or a person experiencing a challenge, or an animal in need of a forever home - send the angels to bring whatever is needed in that situation.

In your time of meditation or prayer each day, send the angels to assist everyone in need across the planet.

Send them to leaders and those in authority that they would govern with love and compassion. Ask the angels to inspire leaders to put the wellbeing of their people before personal ambition, greed, or the desire for power.

Send angels to Mother Earth for healing and restoration. Ask the angels to protect the planet from human error and the desire for convenience. Ask them to restore the environment and to protect the plants and animals from pollution and toxic substances in the air, ground, and water.

It may seem like a simple thing to do, but the effects are more powerful and effective than we will ever know. The angels stand ready to serve, and they willingly act – as long as we ask in accordance with Divine Love, and that means asking only for good.

We do offer this one observation: Once you connect with the angels, your life will never quite be the same. We pray that you too will experience the richness, the blessings, the happy surprises that come when you begin to walk with your angels. Life will never be boring.

If you enjoyed this book. Please leave us a great review on Amazon. Your help will assist us in getting the book into the hands of those who wish to know more about angels.

You will find us on facebook:

https://www.facebook.com/TheAngelLadies/

Also, visit the website www.theangelladies.com where you'll learn more about what we do and other resources that are available for you. Sign up for our free newsletter.

Blessings in your journey.

Deb and Jean,
The Angel Ladies

www.theangelladies.com

Manufactured by Amazon.ca
Bolton, ON

11848051R00070